Nmap® Cookbook

The fat-free guide to network scanning

Nmap® Cookbook
The Fat-free Guide to Network Scanning

Copyright © 2010 Nicholas Marsh
All rights reserved.

ISBN: 1449902529
EAN-13: 9781449902520

www.NmapCookbook.com

BSD® is a registered trademark of the University of California, Berkeley
CentOS is property of CentOS Ltd.
Debian® is a registered trademark of Software in the Public Interest, Inc
Fedora® is a registered trademark of Red Hat, Inc.
FreeBSD® is a registered trademark of The FreeBSD Foundation
Gentoo® is a registered trademark of The Gentoo Foundation
Linux® is the registered trademark of Linus Torvalds
Mac OS X® is a registered trademark of Apple, Inc.
Windows® is a registered trademark of Microsoft Corporation
Nmap® is a registered trademark of Insecure.Com LLC
Red Hat® is a registered trademark of Red Hat, Inc.
Ubuntu® is a registered trademark of Canonical Ltd.
UNIX® is a registered trademark of The Open Group

All other trademarks used in this book are property of their respective owners. Use of any trademark in this book does not constitute an affiliation with or endorsement from the trademark holder.

All information in this book is presented on an "as-is" basis. No warranty or guarantee is provided and the author and/or publisher shall not be held liable for any loss or damage.

Contents at a Glance

Introduction 15

Section 1: Installing Nmap 19

Section 2: Basic Scanning Techniques 33

Section 3: Discovery Options 45

Section 4: Advanced Scanning Options 65

Section 5: Port Scanning Options 79

Section 6: Operating System and Service Detection 89

Section 7: Timing Options 97

Section 8: Evading Firewalls 115

Section 9: Output Options 127

Section 10: Troubleshooting and Debugging 135

Section 11: Zenmap 147

Section 12: Nmap Scripting Engine (NSE) 161

Section 13: Ndiff 171

Section 14: Tips and Tricks 177

Appendix A - Nmap Cheat Sheet 187

Appendix B - Nmap Port States 191

Appendix C - CIDR Cross Reference 193

Appendix D - Common TCP/IP Ports 195

Table of Contents

Introduction 15
    Conventions Used In This Book 18
Section 1: Installing Nmap 19
    Installation Overview 20
    Installing Nmap on Windows 21
    Installing Nmap on Unix and Linux systems 25
        Installing Precompiled Packages for Linux 25
        Compiling Nmap from Source for Unix and Linux 26
    Installing Nmap on Mac OS X 29
Section 2: Basic Scanning Techniques 33
    Basic Scanning Overview 34
    Scan a Single Target 35
    Scan Multiple Targets 36
    Scan a Range of IP Addresses 37
    Scan an Entire Subnet 38
    Scan a List of Targets 39
    Scan Random Targets 40
    Exclude Targets from a Scan 41
    Exclude Targets Using a List 42
    Perform an Aggressive Scan 43
    Scan an IPv6 Target 44
Section 3: Discovery Options 45
    Discovery Options Overview 46
    Don't Ping 47
    Ping Only Scan 48
    TCP SYN Ping 49
    TCP ACK Ping 50
    UDP Ping 51
    SCTP INIT Ping 52

ICMP Echo Ping 53

ICMP Timestamp Ping 54

ICMP Address Mask Ping 55

IP Protocol Ping 56

ARP Ping 57

Traceroute 58

Force Reverse DNS Resolution 59

Disable Reverse DNS Resolution 60

Alternative DNS Lookup Method 61

Manually Specify DNS Server(s) 62

Create a Host List 63

Section 4: Advanced Scanning Options 65

Advanced Scanning Functions Overview 66

TCP SYN Scan 67

TCP Connect Scan 68

UDP Scan 69

TCP NULL Scan 70

TCP FIN Scan 71

Xmas Scan 72

Custom TCP Scan 73

TCP ACK Scan 74

IP Protocol Scan 75

Send Raw Ethernet Packets 76

Send IP Packets 77

Section 5: Port Scanning Options 79

Port Scanning Options Overview 80

Perform a Fast Scan 81

Scan Specific Ports 82

Scan Ports by Name 83

Scan Ports by Protocol 84

Scan All Ports 85

Scan Top Ports 86

Perform a Sequential Port Scan 87

Section 6: Operating System and Service Detection 89

Version Detection Overview 90

Operating System Detection 91

Submitting TCP/IP Fingerprints 92

Attempt to Guess an Unknown Operating System 93

Service Version Detection 94

Troubleshooting Version Scans 95

Perform an RPC Scan 96

Section 7: Timing Options 97

Timing Options Overview 98

Timing Parameters 99

Timing Templates 100

Minimum Number of Parallel Operations 101

Maximum Number of Parallel Operations 102

Minimum Host Group Size 103

Maximum Host Group Size 104

Initial RTT Timeout 105

Maximum RTT Timeout 106

Maximum Retries 107

Set the Packet TTL 108

Host Timeout 109

Minimum Scan Delay 110

Maximum Scan Delay 111

Minimum Packet Rate 112

Maximum Packet Rate 113

Defeat Reset Rate Limits 114

Section 8: Evading Firewalls 115

Firewall Evasion Techniques Overview 116

Fragment Packets 117

Specify a Specific MTU 118

Use a Decoy 119

Idle Zombie Scan 120

Manually Specify a Source Port Number 121

Append Random Data 122

Randomize Target Scan Order 123

Spoof MAC Address 124

Send Bad Checksums 125

Section 9: Output Options 127

Output Options Overview 128

Save Output to a Text File 129

Save Output to a XML File 130

Grepable Output 131

Output All Supported File Types 132

Display Scan Statistics 133

133t Output 134

Section 10: Troubleshooting and Debugging 135

Troubleshooting and Debugging Overview 136

Getting Help 137

Display Nmap Version 138

Verbose Output 139

Debugging 140

Display Port State Reason Codes 141

Only Display Open Ports 142

Trace Packets 143

Display Host Networking Configuration 144

Specify Which Network Interface to Use 145

Section 11: Zenmap 147

Zenmap Overview 148

Launching Zenmap 149

Basic Zenmap Operations 150

Zenmap Results 151

Scanning Profiles 152

Profile Editor 153

Viewing Open Ports 154

Viewing a Network Map 155

Saving Network Maps 156

Viewing Host Details 157

Viewing Scan History 158

Comparing Scan Results 159

Saving Scans 160

Section 12: Nmap Scripting Engine (NSE) 161

Nmap Scripting Engine Overview 162

Execute Individual Scripts 163

Execute Multiple Scripts 164

Script Categories 165

Execute Scripts by Category 166

Execute Multiple Script Categories 167

Troubleshoot Scripts 168

Update the Script Database 169

Section 13: Ndiff 171

Ndiff Overview 172

Scan Comparison Using Ndiff 173

Ndiff Verbose Mode 174

XML Output Mode 175

Section 14: Tips and Tricks 177

Tips and Tricks Overview 178

11

Combine Multiple Options 179

Scan Using Interactive Mode 180

Runtime Interaction 181

Remotely Scan Your Network 182

Wireshark 183

Scanme.Insecure.org 184

Nmap Online Resources 185

Appendix A - Nmap Cheat Sheet 187

Appendix B - Nmap Port States 191

Appendix C - CIDR Cross Reference 193

Appendix D - Common TCP/IP Ports 195

This guide is dedicated to the open source community. Without the tireless efforts of open source developers, programs like Nmap would not exist. Many of these developers devote large amounts of their spare time creating and supporting wonderful open source applications and ask for nothing in return.

The collaborative manner in which open source software is developed shows the true potential of humanity if we all work together towards a common goal.

Introduction

Nmap is an open source program released under the GNU General Public License (see www.gnu.org/copyleft/gpl.html). It is an evaluable tool for network administrators which can be used to discover, monitor, and troubleshoot TCP/IP systems. Nmap is a free cross-platform network scanning utility created by Gordon "Fyodor" Lyon and is actively developed by a community of volunteers.

```
nick@d630:~$ sudo nmap -A 192.168.10.100

Starting Nmap 5.00 ( http://nmap.org ) at 2009-12-12 21:23 CST
Interesting ports on 192.168.10.100:
Not shown: 999 closed ports
PORT    STATE SERVICE VERSION
22/tcp  open  ssh     OpenSSH 5.1p1 Debian 5ubuntu1 (protocol 2.0)
Device type: general purpose
Running: Linux 2.6.X
OS details: Linux 2.6.17 - 2.6.28
Network Distance: 0 hops
Service Info: OS: Linux

OS and Service detection performed. Please report any incorrect resu
lts at http://nmap.org/submit/ .
Nmap done: 1 IP address (1 host up) scanned in 1.77 seconds
nick@d630:~$
```

A typical Nmap scan

Nmap's award-winning suite of network scanning utilities has been in constant development since 1997 and continually improves with each new release. Version 5.00 of Nmap (released in July of 2009) adds many new features and enhancements including:

- Improved service and operating system version detection (see page 89)
- Improved support for Windows and Mac OS X
- Improved Nmap Scripting Engine (NSE) for performing complex scanning tasks (see page 161)
- Addition of the Ndiff utility which can be used to compare Nmap scans (see page 171)

- Ability to graphically display network topology with Zenmap (see page 147)
- Additional language localizations including German, French, and Portuguese.
- Better overall performance

The Nmap project relies on volunteers to support and develop this amazing tool. If you would like to help improve Nmap, there are several ways to get involved:

Promote Nmap

Nmap is a wonderful tool that every administrator network should know about. Despite its popularity, Nmap isn't widely known outside of technically elite circles. Promote Nmap by introducing it to your friends or write a blog entry about it and help spread the word.

Report Bugs

You can help improve Nmap by reporting any bugs you discover to the Nmap developers. The Nmap project provides a mailing list for this which can be found online at www.seclists.org/nmap-dev.

> **Note** *Thousands of people worldwide use Nmap. Additionally, Nmap developers are very busy people. Before reporting a bug, or asking for assistance, you should search the Nmap website at www.insecure.org/search.html to make sure your problem hasn't already been reported or resolved.*

Contribute Code

If you're a hacker with some spare time on your hands, you can get involved with Nmap development. To learn more about contributing code to the Nmap project visit www.nmap.org/data/HACKING.

Submit TCP/IP Fingerprints

If you're not a programmer, you can still improve Nmap by submitting any unknown TCP/IP fingerprints you discover while scanning. The process for this is discussed on page 92. Submitting fingerprints is easy and it helps improve Nmap's software version and operating system detection capabilities. Visit www.nmap.org/submit/ for more information or to submit your discoveries.

Sponsor Nmap

The Nmap project does not accept donations. If, however, you have a security related service you would like promote, you can sponsor Nmap by purchasing an advertising package on the insecure.org website. For more information visit www.insecure.org/advertising.html.

Conventions Used In This Book

```
C:\>nmap scanme.insecure.org
```
Nmap running on Microsoft Windows systems

```
$ nmap scanme.insecure.org
```
Nmap running on non-privileged account for Unix/Linux/Mac OS X

```
# nmap scanme.insecure.org
```
Nmap running on Unix/Linux/Mac OS X systems as the root user

```
$ sudo nmap scanme.insecure.org
```
Using the sudo command to elevate privileges for Unix/Linux/Mac OS X

Note: *Windows users may omit the **sudo** command where used in examples as its use is not necessary and will not work on Microsoft based systems.*

```
# nmap -T2 scanme.insecure.org
```
Using command line arguments with Nmap

Important: *Nmap's command line arguments are <u>case sensitive</u>. The **-T2** option (see page 100) in the example above is not the same as **-t2** and will result in an error if specified in the incorrect case.*

```
...
```
Additional Nmap output truncated (to save space)

Section 1:
Installing Nmap

Installation Overview

Nmap has its roots in the Unix and Linux environment, but has recently become more compatible with both Microsoft Windows and Apple's Mac OS X operating system. While great care is taken to make Nmap a universal experience on every platform, the reality is that you may experience bugs, errors, and performance issues when using Nmap on a non-traditional system. This applies mainly to Windows and Mac OS X systems which have various idiosyncrasies that are not present on a typical Unix or Linux system.

Author's note: *The Windows port of Nmap has greatly improved with Nmap 5.0. Increases in performance and reliability make Nmap for Windows as reliable as its Linux counterpart. Unfortunately, the Mac OS port is still a little rough around the edges. Many of the problems with Nmap on Mac OS X stem from issues in Apple's latest release (Mac OS X 10.6). From monitoring the Nmap developers list, I can confirm that developers are aware of these issues and working to resolve them. These issues will no doubt be resolved over time as development of Nmap version 5.00 continues.*

Skip ahead for installation procedures for your platform:

Installing Nmap on Windows	Page 21
Installing Nmap on Linux	Page 25
Installing Nmap from source (Unix and Linux)	Page 26
Installing Nmap on Mac OS X	Page 29

Installing Nmap on Windows

Step 1

Download the Windows version of Nmap from www.nmap.org.

Step 2

Launch the Nmap setup program. Select the default installation (recommended) which will install the entire Nmap suite of utilities.

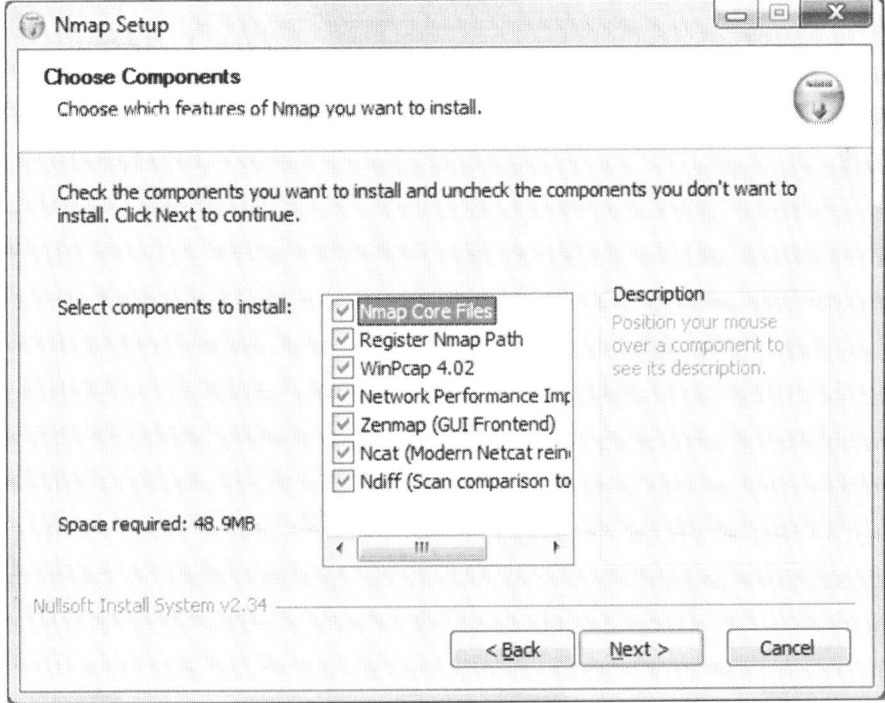

Nmap for Windows installer

Step 3

During installation, a helper program called WinPcap will also be installed. WinPcap is required for Nmap to function properly on the Windows platform so do not skip this step.

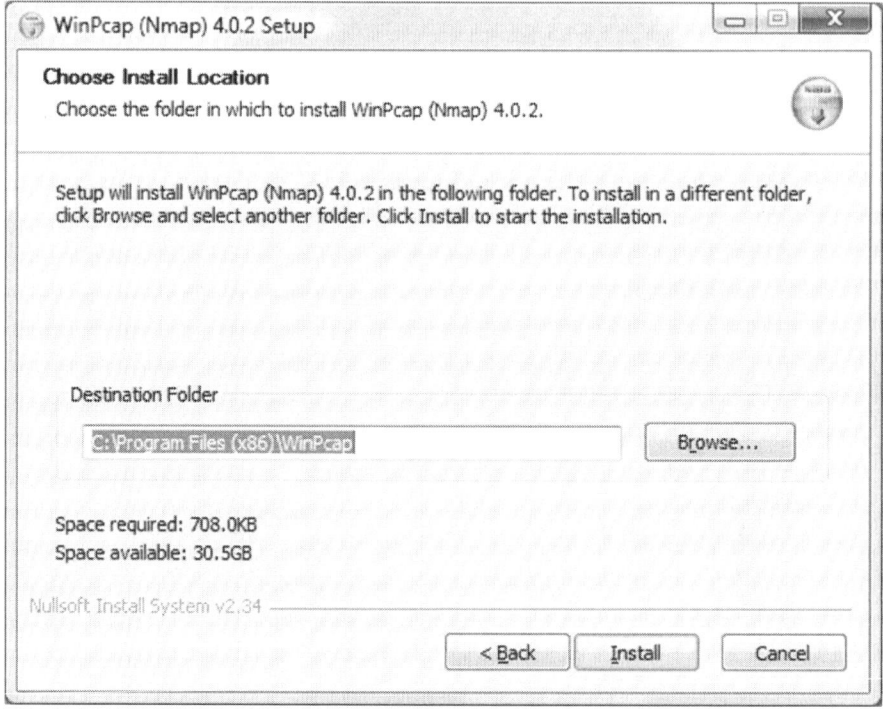

WinPcap for Windows installer

Step 4

After the WinPcap installation has completed you are given the option to configure its service settings. The default options will enable the WinPcap service to start when Windows boots. This is recommended as Nmap will not function correctly when the WinPcap service is not running.

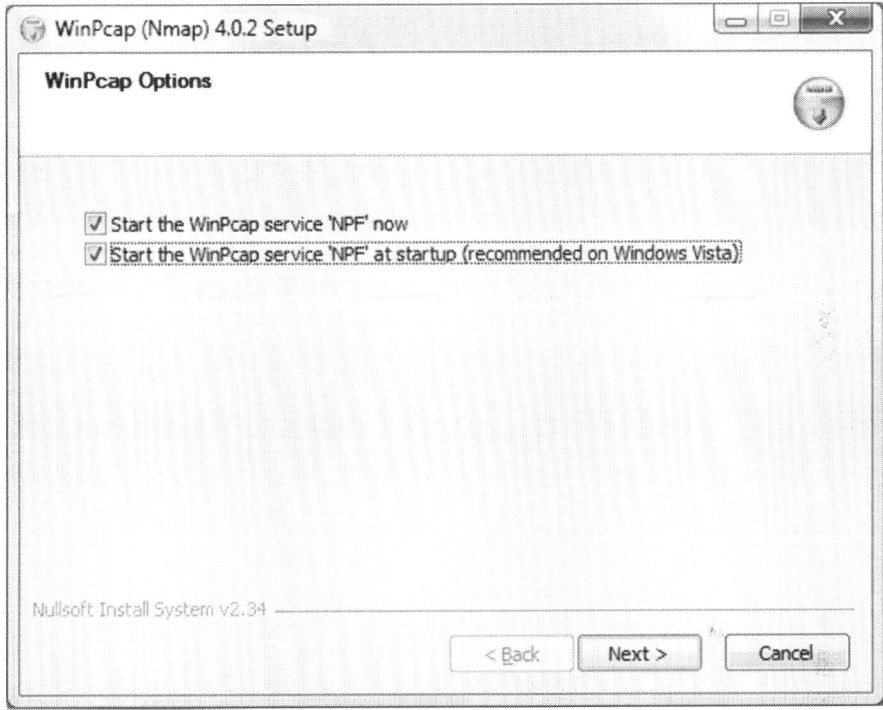

WinPcap settings

Step 5

Once Nmap has been successfully installed you can verify it is working correctly by executing **nmap scanme.insecure.org** on the command line (located in **Start > Programs > Accessories > Command Prompt**).

```
C:\>nmap scanme.insecure.org

Starting Nmap 5.00 ( http://nmap.org ) at 2009-08-07 09:36 Central
Daylight Time

Interesting ports on scanme.nmap.org (64.13.134.52):
Not shown: 994 filtered ports
PORT       STATE  SERVICE
25/tcp     closed smtp
70/tcp     closed gopher
80/tcp     open   http
110/tcp    closed pop3
113/tcp    closed auth
31337/tcp  closed Elite

Nmap done: 1 IP address (1 host up) scanned in 9.25 seconds
C:\>
```

Nmap test scan on Microsoft Windows

If the results of your scan are similar to the results above, then you have successfully installed Nmap. If you receive an error, refer to Section 10 of this book for troubleshooting and debugging information.

Installing Nmap on Unix and Linux systems

Most popular Linux distributions provide binary Nmap packages which allow for simple installation. Installation on Unix systems requires compiling Nmap from source code (as described on page 26).

> **Note:** At the time of this writing Nmap version 5.00 was not available for automatic installation on some Linux distributions. For many, installing Nmap via the popular **apt** or **yum** package managers will only install version 4.x. If your distribution already has Nmap 5.00 in their repositories you can install Nmap by using the commands listed below. Otherwise, refer to page 26 to install Nmap 5.00 from source code.

Installing Precompiled Packages for Linux

For Debian and Ubuntu based systems

```
# apt-get install nmap
```

For Red Hat and Fedora based systems

```
# yum install nmap
```

For Gentoo Linux based systems

```
# emerge nmap
```

To check which version of Nmap you are running, type the following command on the command line:

```
# nmap -V
Nmap version 5.00 ( http://nmap.org )
```

25

Compiling Nmap from Source for Unix and Linux

Currently, the only way to get Nmap 5.00 for most Unix and Linux systems is to download and compile the source code from the nmap.org website. Building Nmap from source takes a little extra work, but is well worth the effort to get the new features in Nmap's latest release. The following five steps detail the procedure for installing Nmap from source.

Step 1

Download the Nmap 5.00 source from www.nmap.org/download.html. This can be done via a standard web browser or from the command line using the *wget* command found on most Unix based systems.

```
$ wget http://nmap.org/dist/nmap-5.00.tgz
--2009-08-06 19:29:35--  http://nmap.org/dist/nmap-5.00.tgz
Resolving nmap.org... 64.13.134.48
Connecting to nmap.org|64.13.134.48|:80... connected.
HTTP request sent, awaiting response... 200 OK
Length: 9902346 (9.4M) [application/x-tar]
Saving to: `nmap-5.00.tgz'

100%[===================================>] 9,902,346  1.39M/s   in 7.5s
2009-08-06 19:29:42 (1.27 MB/s) - `nmap-5.00.tgz' saved [9902346/9902346]
```

Downloading Nmap on Unix and Linux systems via the command line

Step 2

Extract the contents of the Nmap package by typing **tar -xf nmap-5.00.tgz**.

```
$ tar -xf nmap-5.00.tgz
...
```

Extracting Nmap source code

Step 3

Configure and build the Nmap source code by typing **cd nmap-5.00/** and then **./configure && make** on the command line.

```
$ cd nmap-5.00/
$ ./configure && make
checking build system type... x86_64-unknown-linux-gnu
checking host system type... x86_64-unknown-linux-gnu
checking for gcc... gcc
checking for C compiler default output file name... a.out
checking whether the C compiler works... yes
...
```

Compiling Nmap source code

Step 4

Install the compiled code by typing **sudo make install** on the command line.

> **Note** This step will require root privileges. You must login as the root user or use the **sudo** command to complete this step.

```
$ sudo make install
Password: ********
/usr/bin/install -c -d /usr/local/bin /usr/local/share/man/man1
/usr/local/share/nmap
/usr/bin/install -c -c -m 755 nmap /usr/local/bin/nmap
/usr/bin/strip -x /usr/local/bin/nmap
/usr/bin/install -c -c -m 644 docs/nmap.1 /usr/local/share/man/man1/
/usr/bin/install -c -c -m 644 docs/nmap.xsl /usr/local/share/nmap/
...
NMAP SUCCESSFULLY INSTALLED
$
```

Installing Nmap from source code

Step 5

Once Nmap has been successfully installed, you can verify it is working correctly by executing **nmap localhost** on the command line.

```
$ nmap localhost
Starting Nmap 5.00 ( http://nmap.org ) at 2009-08-07 00:42 CDT
Warning: Hostname localhost resolves to 2 IPs. Using 127.0.0.1.
Interesting ports on e6400 (127.0.0.1):
Not shown: 993 closed ports
PORT       STATE   SERVICE
22/tcp     open    ssh
25/tcp     open    smtp
111/tcp    open    rpcbind
139/tcp    open    netbios-ssn
445/tcp    open    microsoft-ds
631/tcp    open    ipp
2049/tcp   open    nfs

Nmap done: 1 IP address (1 host up) scanned in 0.20 seconds
```

Nmap test scan on Unix/Linux

If the results of your scan are similar to the results above, then you have successfully installed Nmap. If you receive an error, refer to Section 10 of this book for troubleshooting and debugging information.

Installing Nmap on Mac OS X

Step 1

Download the Mac OS X version of Nmap from www.nmap.org.

> **Note:** *Nmap 5.00 for Mac OS X is a universal installer that works on both Intel and PowerPC Macintosh systems.*

Step 2

Launch the Nmap setup program and click *continue*. Then, accept the license terms of the Nmap program.

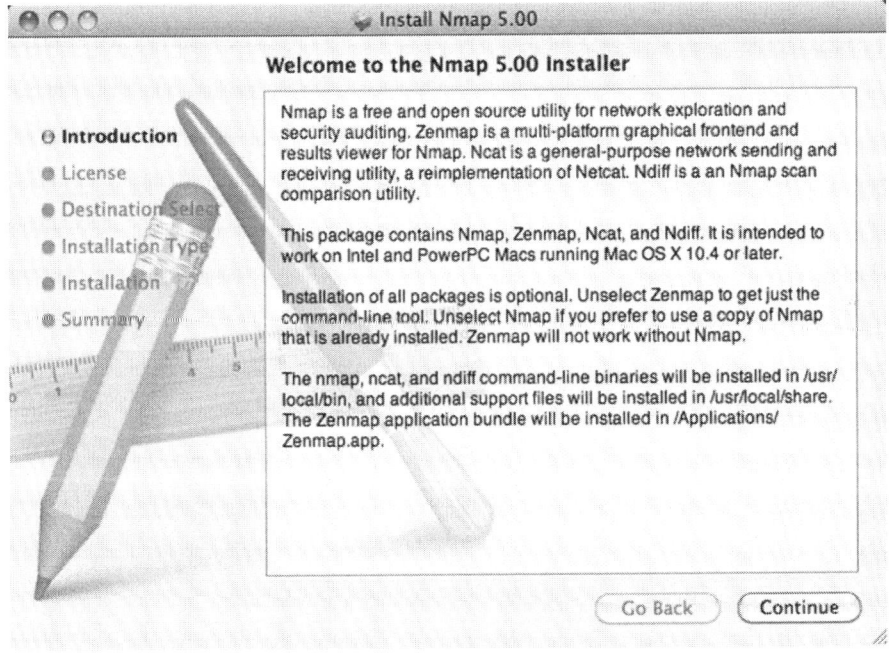

Nmap for Mac OS X installer

Step 3

When prompted for the installation options, leave the default selections checked (recommended). This will install the entire Nmap suite of utilities. Click *continue* to begin the installation process.

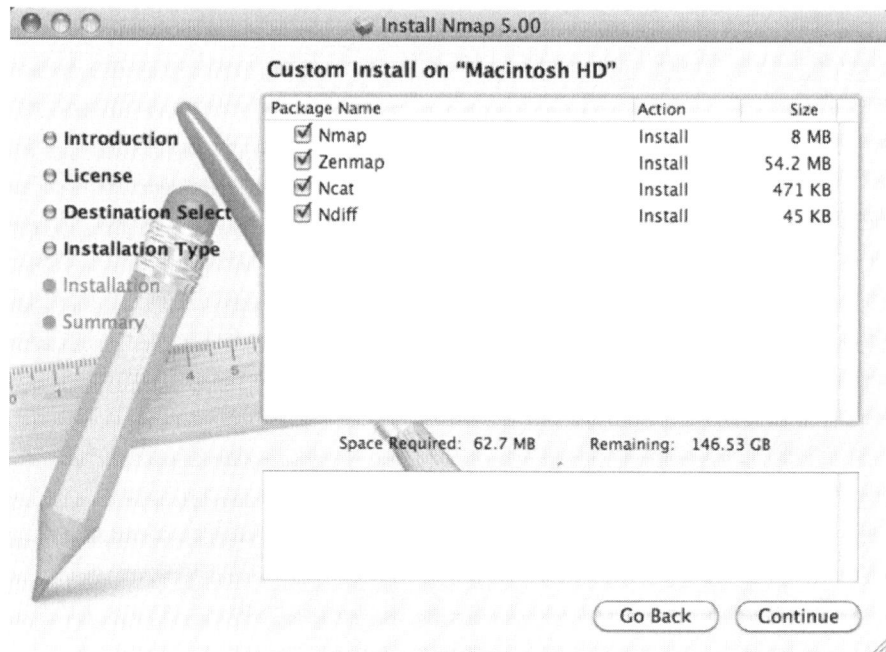

Default installation settings

Step 4

When the installation is complete you can close the Nmap installer.

Successful installation of Nmap on Mac OS X

Step 5

Once Nmap has been successfully installed, you can verify it is working correctly by executing **nmap localhost** in the Mac OS X Terminal application (located in **Applications > Utilities > Terminal**).

```
Last login: Fri Dec 11 12:16:44 on ttys000
$ nmap -V

Nmap version 5.00 ( http://nmap.org )
$ nmap localhost

Starting Nmap 5.00 ( http://nmap.org ) at 2009-12-11 12:17 CST
Interesting ports on localhost (127.0.0.1):
Not shown: 999 closed ports
PORT     STATE SERVICE
631/tcp  open  ipp

Nmap done: 1 IP address (1 host up) scanned in 7.36 seconds
$
```

Nmap test scan on Mac OS X

If the results of your scan are similar to the results above, then you have successfully installed Nmap. If you receive an error, refer to Section 10 of this book for troubleshooting and debugging information.

Section 2:

Basic Scanning Techniques

Basic Scanning Overview

This section covers the basics of network scanning with Nmap. Before we begin it is important to understand the following concepts:

- Firewalls, routers, proxy servers, and other security devices can skew the results of an Nmap scan. Scanning remote hosts that are not on your local network may provide misleading information because of this.
- Some scanning options require elevated privileges. On Unix and Linux systems you may be required to login as the root user or to execute Nmap using the **sudo** command.

There are also several warnings to take into consideration:

- Scanning networks that you do not have permission to scan can get you in trouble with your internet service provider, the police, and possibly even the government. Don't go off scanning the FBI or Secret Service websites unless you want to get in trouble.
- Aggressively scanning some systems may cause them to crash which can lead to undesirable results like system downtime and data loss. Always scan mission critical systems with caution.

Now let's start scanning!

Scan a Single Target

Executing Nmap with no command line options will perform a basic scan on the specified target. A target can be specified as an IP address or host name (which Nmap will try to resolve).

Usage syntax: nmap [target]

```
$ nmap 192.168.10.1

Starting Nmap 5.00 ( http://nmap.org ) at 2009-08-07 19:38 CDT
Interesting ports on 192.168.10.1:
Not shown: 997 filtered ports
PORT    STATE  SERVICE
20/tcp  closed ftp-data
21/tcp  closed ftp
80/tcp  open   http

Nmap done: 1 IP address (1 host up) scanned in 7.21 seconds
```

Single target scan

The resulting scan shows the status of ports detected on the specified target. The table below describes the output fields displayed by the scan.

PORT	STATE	SERVICE
Port number/protocol	Status of the port	Type of service for the port

A default Nmap scan will check for the 1000 most commonly used TCP/IP ports. Ports that respond to a probe are classified into one of six port states: open, closed, filtered, unfiltered, open|filtered, closed|filtered. See Appendix B for more information about port states.

35

Scan Multiple Targets

Nmap can be used to scan multiple hosts at the same time. The easiest way to do this is to string together the target IP addresses or host names on the command line (separated by a space).

Usage syntax: nmap [target1 target2 etc]

```
$ nmap 192.168.10.1 192.168.10.100 192.168.10.101

Starting Nmap 5.00 ( http://nmap.org ) at 2009-08-07 20:30 CDT
Interesting ports on 192.168.10.1:
Not shown: 997 filtered ports
PORT     STATE  SERVICE
20/tcp   closed ftp-data
21/tcp   closed ftp
80/tcp   open   http

Interesting ports on 192.168.10.100:
Not shown: 995 closed ports
PORT      STATE SERVICE
22/tcp    open  ssh
111/tcp   open  rpcbind
139/tcp   open  netbios-ssn
445/tcp   open  microsoft-ds
2049/tcp  open  nfs

Nmap done: 3 IP addresses (2 hosts up) scanned in 6.23 seconds
```

Multiple target scan

The example above demonstrates using Nmap to scan three addresses at the same time.

| Tip | Since all three targets in the above example are on the same subnet you could use the shorthand notation of **nmap 192.168.10.1,100,101** to achieve the same results. |

Scan a Range of IP Addresses

A range of IP addresses can be used for target specification as demonstrated in the example below.

Usage syntax: nmap [Range of IP addresses]

```
$ nmap 192.168.10.1-100

Starting Nmap 5.00 ( http://nmap.org ) at 2009-08-07 20:40 CDT
Interesting ports on 192.168.10.1:
Not shown: 997 filtered ports
PORT      STATE  SERVICE
20/tcp    closed ftp-data
21/tcp    closed ftp
80/tcp    open   http

Interesting ports on 192.168.10.100:
Not shown: 995 closed ports
PORT      STATE  SERVICE
22/tcp    open   ssh
111/tcp   open   rpcbind
139/tcp   open   netbios-ssn
445/tcp   open   microsoft-ds

Nmap done: 100 IP addresses (2 hosts up) scanned in 25.84 seconds
```

Scanning a range of IP addresses

In this example Nmap is instructed to scan the range of IP addresses from 192.168.10.1 through 192.168.10.100. You can also use ranges to scan multiple networks/subnets. For example typing **nmap 192.168.1-100.*** would scan the class C IP networks of 192.168.1.* through 192.168.100.*.

> **Note** *The asterisk is a wildcard character which represents all valid ranges from 0-255.*

Scan an Entire Subnet

Nmap can be used to scan an entire subnet using CIDR (Classless Inter-Domain Routing) notation.

Usage syntax: nmap [Network/CIDR]

```
$ nmap 192.168.10.1/24

Starting Nmap 5.00 ( http://nmap.org ) at 2009-08-07 20:43 CDT
Interesting ports on 192.168.10.1:
Not shown: 996 filtered ports
PORT     STATE  SERVICE
20/tcp   closed ftp-data
21/tcp   closed ftp
23/tcp   closed telnet
80/tcp   open   http

Interesting ports on 192.168.10.100:
Not shown: 995 closed ports
PORT     STATE SERVICE
22/tcp   open  ssh
111/tcp  open  rpcbind
139/tcp  open  netbios-ssn
445/tcp  open  microsoft-ds
2049/tcp open  nfs

Nmap done: 256 IP addresses (2 hosts up) scanned in 8.78 second
```

Scanning an entire class C subnet using CDIR notation

The above example instructs Nmap to scan the entire 192.168.10.0 network using CIDR notation. CIDR notation consists of the network address and subnet mask (in binary bits) separated by a slash. See Appendix C for a cross reference of subnet masks and their CIDR notations.

Scan a List of Targets

If you have a large number of systems to scan, you can enter the IP address (or host names) in a text file and use that file as input for Nmap on the command line.

```
$ cat list.txt
192.168.10.1
192.168.10.100
192.168.10.101
```

Target IP addresses in a text file

The list.txt file above contains a list of hosts to be scanned. Each entry in the list.txt file must be separated by a space, tab, or newline. The **-iL** parameter is used to instruct Nmap to extract the list of targets from the list.txt file.

Usage syntax: nmap -iL [list.txt]

```
$ nmap -iL list.txt

Starting Nmap 5.00 ( http://nmap.org ) at 2009-08-07 19:44 CDT
Interesting ports on 192.168.10.1:
Not shown: 997 filtered ports
PORT     STATE  SERVICE
20/tcp   closed ftp-data
21/tcp   closed ftp
80/tcp   open   http

Interesting ports on 192.168.10.100:
Not shown: 995 closed ports
PORT     STATE  SERVICE
22/tcp   open   ssh
...
```

Nmap scan using a list for target specification

The resulting scan displayed above will be performed for each host in the list.txt file.

Scan Random Targets

The **-iR** parameter can be used to select random internet hosts to scan. Nmap will randomly generate the specified number of targets and attempt to scan them.

Usage syntax: nmap -iR [number of targets]

```
# nmap -iR 3
Starting Nmap 5.00 ( http://nmap.org ) at 2009-08-07 23:40 CDT
...
Nmap done: 3 IP addresses (2 hosts up) scanned in 36.91 seconds
```
Scanning three randomly generated IP addresses

> **Note** *For privacy reasons we do not display the results of the above scan in this book.*

Executing **nmap -iR 3** instructs Nmap to randomly generate 3 IP addresses to scan. There aren't many good reasons to ever do a random scan unless you are working on a research project (or just really bored). Additionally, if you do a lot of aggressive random scanning you could end up getting in trouble with your internet service provider.

Exclude Targets from a Scan

The **--exclude** option is used with Nmap to exclude hosts from a scan.

Usage syntax: nmap [targets] --exclude [target(s)]

```
$ nmap 192.168.10.0/24 --exclude 192.168.10.100

Starting Nmap 5.00 ( http://nmap.org ) at 2009-08-08 20:39 CDT
Interesting ports on 192.168.10.1:
Not shown: 996 filtered ports
PORT    STATE  SERVICE
20/tcp  closed ftp-data
21/tcp  closed ftp
23/tcp  closed telnet
80/tcp  open   http
...
```

Excluding a single IP from a scan

The **--exclude** option is useful if you want to exclude specific hosts when scanning a large number of addresses. In the example above host 192.168.10.100 is excluded from the range of targets being scanned.

The **--exclude** option accepts single hosts, ranges, or entire network blocks (using CIDR notation) as demonstrated in the next example.

```
$ nmap 192.168.10.0/24 --exclude 192.168.10.100-105

Starting Nmap 5.00 ( http://nmap.org ) at 2009-08-08 20:39 CDT
...
```

Excluding a range of IP addresses from a scan

Exclude Targets Using a List

The **--excludefile** option is similar to the **--exclude** option and can be used to provide a list of targets to exclude from a network scan.

```
$ cat list.txt
192.168.10.1
192.168.10.12
192.168.10.44
```

Text file with hosts to exclude from a scan

The example below demonstrates using the **--excludefile** argument to exclude the hosts in the list.txt file displayed above.

Usage syntax: nmap [targets] --excludefile [list.txt]

```
$ nmap 192.168.10.0/24 --excludefile list.txt

Starting Nmap 5.00 ( http://nmap.org ) at 2009-08-08 20:49 CDT
Interesting ports on 192.168.10.100:
Not shown: 995 closed ports
PORT      STATE SERVICE
22/tcp    open  ssh
111/tcp   open  rpcbind
139/tcp   open  netbios-ssn
445/tcp   open  microsoft-ds
2049/tcp  open  nfs

Nmap done: 253 IP addresses (1 host up) scanned in 33.10 second
```

Excluding a list of hosts from a network scan

In the above example, the targets in the list.txt file are excluded from the scan.

Perform an Aggressive Scan

The **-A** parameter instructs Nmap to perform an aggressive scan.

Usage syntax: nmap -A [target]

```
# nmap -A 10.10.1.51

Starting Nmap 5.00 ( http://nmap.org ) at 2009-08-10 09:39 CDT
Interesting ports on 10.10.1.51:
Not shown: 999 closed ports
PORT   STATE SERVICE VERSION
80/tcp open  http    Linksys WAP54G wireless-G router http config
|_ html-title: 401 Unauthorized
| http-auth: HTTP Service requires authentication
|_  Auth type: Basic, realm = Linksys WAP54G
MAC Address: 00:12:17:AA:66:28 (Cisco-Linksys)
Device type: general purpose
Running: Linux 2.4.X
OS details: Linux 2.4.18 - 2.4.35 (likely embedded)
Network Distance: 1 hop
Service Info: Device: WAP

OS and Service detection performed. Please report any incorrect
results at http://nmap.org/submit/ .
Nmap done: 1 IP address (1 host up) scanned in 9.61 seconds
```

Output of an aggressive scan

The aggressive scan selects some of the most commonly used options within Nmap and is provided as a simple alternative to typing a long string of command line arguments. The **-A** parameter is a synonym for several advanced options (like **-O -sC --traceroute**) which can also be accessed individually and are covered later in this book.

Scan an IPv6 Target

The **-6** parameter is used to perform a scan of an IP version 6 target.

Usage syntax: nmap -6 [target]

```
# nmap -6 fe80::29aa:9db9:4164:d80e

Starting Nmap 5.00 ( http://nmap.org ) at 2009-08-11 15:52 Central
Daylight Time

Interesting ports on fe80::29aa:9db9:4164:d80e:
Not shown: 993 closed ports
PORT        STATE  SERVICE
135/tcp     open   msrpc
445/tcp     open   microsoft-ds
5357/tcp    open   unknown
49152/tcp   open   unknown
49153/tcp   open   unknown
49154/tcp   open   unknown
49155/tcp   open   unknown

Nmap done: 1 IP address (1 host up) scanned in 227.32 seconds
```

Scanning an IPv6 address

The example above displays the results of scanning an IP version 6 target. Most Nmap options support IPv6 with the exception of multiple target scanning using ranges and CIDR as they are pointless on IPv6 networks.

> **Note** Both the host and the target systems must support the IPv6 protocol in order for a **-6** scan to work.

Section 3:

Discovery Options

Discovery Options Overview

Before port scanning a target, Nmap will attempt to send ICMP echo requests to see if the host is "alive." This can save time when scanning multiple hosts as Nmap will not waste time attempting to probe hosts that are not online. Because ICMP requests are often blocked by firewalls, Nmap will also attempt to connect to port 80 and 443 since these common web server ports are often open (even if ICMP is not).

The default discovery options aren't useful when scanning secured systems and can hinder scanning progress. The following section describes alternative methods for host discovery which allows you to perform more comprehensive discovery when looking for available targets.

Summary of features covered in this section:

Feature	Option
Don't Ping	-PN
Perform a Ping Only Scan	-sP
TCP SYN Ping	-PS
TCP ACK Ping	-PA
UDP Ping	-PU
SCTP INIT Ping	-PY
ICMP Echo Ping	-PE
ICMP Timestamp Ping	-PP
ICMP Address Mask Ping	-PM
IP Protocol Ping	-PO
ARP Ping	-PR
Traceroute	--traceroute
Force Reverse DNS Resolution	-R
Disable Reverse DNS Resolution	-n
Alternative DNS Lookup	--system-dns
Manually Specify DNS Server(s)	--dns-servers
Create a Host List	-sL

Don't Ping

By default, before Nmap attempts to scan a system for open ports it will first ping the target to see if it is online. This feature helps save time when scanning as it causes targets that do not respond to be skipped.

```
$ nmap 10.10.5.11

Starting Nmap 5.00 ( http://nmap.org ) at 2009-08-13 08:43 CDT
Note: Host seems down. If it is really up, but blocking our ping
probes, try -PN
Nmap done: 1 IP address (0 hosts up) scanned in 3.16 seconds
```
Results of a Nmap scan where the target system is not pingable

In the above example the specified target is not scanned as it does not respond to Nmap's pings. The **-PN** option instructs Nmap to skip the default discovery check and perform a complete port scan on the target. This is useful when scanning hosts that are protected by a firewall that blocks ping probes.

Usage syntax: nmap -PN [target]

```
$ nmap -PN 10.10.5.11

Starting Nmap 5.00 ( http://nmap.org ) at 2009-08-13 08:43 CDT
Interesting ports on 10.10.5.11:
Not shown: 999 filtered ports
PORT      STATE  SERVICE
3389/tcp  open   ms-term-serv

Nmap done: 1 IP address (1 host up) scanned in 6.51 seconds
```
Output of a Nmap scan with ping discovery disabled

By specifying the **-PN** option on the same target, Nmap is able to produce a list of open ports on the unpingable system.

47

Ping Only Scan

The **-sP** option is used to perform a simple ping of the specified host.

Usage syntax: nmap -sP [target]

```
$ nmap -sP 192.168.10.2/24

Starting Nmap 5.00 ( http://nmap.org ) at 2009-08-08 20:54 CDT
Host 192.168.10.1 is up (0.0026s latency).
Host 192.168.10.100 is up (0.00020s latency).
Host 192.168.10.101 is up (0.00026s latency).
Nmap done: 256 IP addresses (3 hosts up) scanned in 3.18 second
```

Output of a ping only scan

This option is useful when you want to perform a quick search of the target network to see which hosts are online without actually scanning the target(s) for open ports. In the above example, all 254 addresses in the 192.168.10.0 subnet are pinged and results from live hosts are displayed.

When scanning a local network, you can execute Nmap with root privileges for additional ping functionality. When doing this, the **-sP** option will perform an ARP ping and return the MAC addresses of the discovered system(s).

Usage syntax: nmap -sP [target]

```
# nmap -sP 192.168.10.2/24

Starting Nmap 5.00 ( http://nmap.org ) at 2009-08-08 21:00 CDT
Host 192.168.10.1 is up (0.0037s latency).
MAC Address: 00:16:B6:BE:6D:1D (Cisco-Linksys)
...
```

Output of a ping only scan (as root)

TCP SYN Ping

The **-PS** option performs a TCP SYN ping.

Usage syntax: nmap -PS[port1,port1,etc] [target]

```
# nmap -PS scanme.insecure.org

Starting Nmap 5.00 ( http://nmap.org ) at 2009-08-16 13:31 CDT
Interesting ports on scanme.nmap.org (64.13.134.52):
Not shown: 995 filtered ports
PORT        STATE   SERVICE
53/tcp      open    domain
70/tcp      closed  gopher
80/tcp      open    http
113/tcp     closed  auth
31337/tcp   closed  Elite

Nmap done: 1 IP address (1 host up) scanned in 27.41 seconds
```

Performing a TCP SYN ping

The TCP SYN ping sends a SYN packet to the target system and listens for a response. This alternative discovery method is useful for systems that are configured to block standard ICMP pings.

> **Note**
> The default port for **-PS** is 80, but others can be specified using the following syntax: **nmap -PS22,25,80,443,etc**.

49

TCP ACK Ping

The **-PA** performs a TCP ACK ping on the specified target.

Usage syntax: nmap -PA[port1,port1,etc] [target]

```
# nmap -PA 192.168.1.254

Starting Nmap 5.00 ( http://nmap.org ) at 2009-08-16 13:31 CDT
Interesting ports on home (192.168.1.254):
Not shown: 998 closed ports
PORT     STATE SERVICE
80/tcp   open  http
443/tcp  open  https
MAC Address: 00:25:3C:5F:5A:89 (2Wire)

Nmap done: 1 IP address (1 host up) scanned in 0.81 seconds
```

Performing a TCP ACK ping

The **-PA** option causes Nmap to send TCP ACK packets to the specified hosts. This method attempts to discover hosts by responding to TCP connections that are nonexistent in an attempt to solicit a response from the target. Like other ping options, it is useful in situations where standard ICMP pings are blocked.

> **Note**
> The default port for **-PA** is 80, but others can be specified using the following syntax: **nmap -PA22,25,80,443,etc**.

50

UDP Ping

The **-PU** option performs a UDP ping on the target system.

Usage syntax: nmap -PU[port1,port1,etc] [target]

```
# nmap -PU 192.168.1.254

Starting Nmap 5.00 ( http://nmap.org ) at 2009-08-16 13:30 CDT
Interesting ports on home (192.168.1.254):
Not shown: 998 closed ports
PORT     STATE SERVICE
80/tcp   open  http
443/tcp  open  https
MAC Address: 00:25:3C:5F:5A:89 (2Wire)

Nmap done: 1 IP address (1 host up) scanned in 0.81 second
```
Performing a UDP ping

This discovery method sends UPD packets in an attempt to solicit a response from a target. While most firewalled systems will block this type of connection, some poorly configured systems may allow it if they are only configured to filter TCP connections.

> **Note**: The default port for **-PU** is 40125. Others can be specified by using the following syntax: **nmap -PU22,25,80,443,etc**.

51

SCTP INIT Ping

The **-PY** parameter instructs Nmap to perform an SCTP INIT ping.

Usage syntax: nmap -PY[port1,port1,etc] [target]

```
# nmap -PY 192.168.1.254

Starting Nmap 5.00 ( http://nmap.org ) at 2009-08-16 13:28 CDT
Interesting ports on home (192.168.1.254):
Not shown: 998 closed ports
PORT     STATE SERVICE
80/tcp   open  http
443/tcp  open  https
MAC Address: 00:25:3C:5F:5A:89 (2Wire)

Nmap done: 1 IP address (1 host up) scanned in 0.79 seconds
```
Performing a SCTP INIT ping

This discovery method attempts to locate hosts using the Stream Control Transmission Protocol (SCTP). SCTP is typically used on systems for IP based telephony.

> **Note** The default port for **-PY** is 80. Others can be specified by using the following syntax: **nmap -PY22,25,80,443,etc**.

ICMP Echo Ping

The **-PE** option performs an ICMP (Internet Control Message Protocol) echo ping on the specified system.

Usage syntax: nmap -PE [target]

```
# nmap -PE 192.168.1.254

Starting Nmap 5.00 ( http://nmap.org ) at 2009-08-16 13:26 CDT
Interesting ports on home (192.168.1.254):
Not shown: 998 closed ports
PORT     STATE SERVICE
80/tcp   open  http
443/tcp  open  https
MAC Address: 00:25:3C:5F:5A:89 (2Wire)

Nmap done: 1 IP address (1 host up) scanned in 1.89 seconds
```

Performing an ICMP echo ping

The **-PE** option sends a standard ICMP ping to the target to see if it replies. This type of discovery works best on local networks where ICMP packets can be transmitted with few restrictions. Many internet hosts, however, are configured not respond to ICMP packets for security reasons.

> **Note** The *-PE* option is automatically implied if no other ping options are specified.

ICMP Timestamp Ping

The **-PP** option performs an ICMP timestamp ping.

Usage syntax: nmap -PP [target]

```
# nmap -PP 192.168.1.254

Starting Nmap 5.00 ( http://nmap.org ) at 2009-08-16 13:27 CDT
Interesting ports on home (192.168.1.254):
Not shown: 998 closed ports
PORT     STATE SERVICE
80/tcp   open  http
443/tcp  open  https
MAC Address: 00:25:3C:5F:5A:89 (2Wire)

Nmap done: 1 IP address (1 host up) scanned in 1.83 seconds
```
Performing an ICMP timestamp ping

While most firewalled systems are configured to block ICMP echo requests, some improperly configured systems may still reply to ICMP timestamp requests. This makes **-PP** useful for attempting to solicit responses from firewalled targets.

ICMP Address Mask Ping

The **-PM** option performs an ICMP address mask ping.

Usage syntax: nmap -PM [target]

```
# nmap -PM 192.168.1.254

Starting Nmap 5.00 ( http://nmap.org ) at 2009-08-16 13:26 CDT
Interesting ports on home (192.168.1.254):
Not shown: 998 closed ports
PORT     STATE SERVICE
80/tcp   open  http
443/tcp  open  https
MAC Address: 00:25:3C:5F:5A:89 (2Wire)

Nmap done: 1 IP address (1 host up) scanned in 1.92 seconds
```

Performing an ICMP address mask ping

This unconventional ICMP query (similar to the **-PP** option) attempts to ping the specified host using alternative ICMP registers. This type of ping can occasionally sneak past a firewall that is configured to block standard echo requests.

IP Protocol Ping

The **-PO** option performs an IP protocol ping.

Usage syntax: `nmap -PO[protocol1,protocol2,etc] [target]`

```
# nmap -PO 10.10.1.48

Starting Nmap 5.00 ( http://nmap.org ) at 2009-08-17 09:38 CDT
Interesting ports on 10.10.1.48:
Not shown: 994 closed ports
PORT      STATE SERVICE
21/tcp    open  ftp
22/tcp    open  ssh
25/tcp    open  smtp
80/tcp    open  http
111/tcp   open  rpcbind
2049/tcp  open  nfs
MAC Address: 00:0C:29:D5:38:F4 (VMware)

Nmap done: 1 IP address (1 host up) scanned in 1.97 seconds
```
Performing an IP protocol ping

An IP protocol ping sends packets with the specified protocol to the target. If no protocols are specified the default protocols 1 (ICMP), 2 (IGMP), and 4 (IP-in-IP) are used. To ping using a custom set of protocols, use the following syntax: **nmap -PO1,2,4,etc.**

> **Note** A complete list of Internet Protocol numbers can be found online at www.iana.org/assignments/protocol-numbers/

ARP Ping

The **-PR** option instructs Nmap to perform an ARP (Address Resolution Protocol) ping on the specified target.

Usage syntax: nmap -PR [target]

```
# nmap -PR 192.168.1.254

Starting Nmap 5.00 ( http://nmap.org ) at 2009-08-16 13:16 CDT
Interesting ports on 192.168.1.254:
Not shown: 998 closed ports
PORT     STATE SERVICE
80/tcp   open  http
443/tcp  open  https
MAC Address: 00:25:3C:5F:5A:89 (2Wire)

Nmap done: 1 IP address (1 host up) scanned in 0.81 seconds
```

Performing an ARP ping

The **-PR** option is automatically implied when scanning the local network. This type of discovery is much faster than the other ping methods described in this guide. It also has the added benefit of being more accurate because LAN hosts can't block ARP requests (even if they are behind a firewall).

> **Note:** *APR scans cannot be performed on targets that are not on your local subnet.*

Traceroute

The **--traceroute** parameter can be use to trace the network path to the specified host.

Usage syntax: nmap --traceroute [target]

```
# nmap --traceroute scanme.insecure.org

Starting Nmap 5.00 ( http://nmap.org ) at 2009-08-16 13:01 CDT
Interesting ports on scanme.nmap.org (64.13.134.52):
Not shown: 996 filtered ports
PORT     STATE  SERVICE
53/tcp   open   domain
70/tcp   closed gopher
80/tcp   open   http
113/tcp  closed auth

TRACEROUTE (using port 113/tcp)
HOP RTT    ADDRESS
1   0.91   home (192.168.1.254)
2   24.40  99-60-32-2.lightspeed.wchtks.sbcglobal.net (99.60.32.2)
3   23.12  76.196.172.4
4   22.69  151.164.94.52
5   32.79  ex3-p12-0.eqdltx.sbcglobal.net (69.220.8.53)
6   32.74  asn2828-XO.eqdltx.sbcglobal.net (151.164.249.134)
...
13  74.90  ip65-46-255-94.z255-46-65.customer.algx.net (65.46.255.94)
14  75.01  scanme.nmap.org (64.13.134.52)

Nmap done: 1 IP address (1 host up) scanned in 33.72 seconds
```

Output of a traceroute scan

The information displayed is similar to the **traceroute** or **tracepath** commands found on Unix and Linux systems - with the added bonus of Nmap's tracing being functionally superior to these commands.

Force Reverse DNS Resolution

The **-R** parameter instructs Nmap to always perform reverse DNS resolution on the target IP address.

Usage syntax: nmap -R [target]

```
# nmap -R 64.13.134.52

Starting Nmap 5.00 ( http://nmap.org ) at 2009-08-13 17:22 Central
Daylight Time

Interesting ports on scanme.nmap.org (64.13.134.52):
Not shown: 993 filtered ports
PORT       STATE  SERVICE
25/tcp     closed smtp
53/tcp     open   domain
70/tcp     closed gopher
80/tcp     open   http
110/tcp    closed pop3
113/tcp    closed auth
31337/tcp  closed Elite

Nmap done: 1 IP address (1 host up) scanned in 9.38 seconds
```

Output of a Nmap scan with reverse DNS enabled

By default, Nmap will only do reverse DNS for hosts that appear to be online. The **-R** option is useful when performing reconnaissance on a block of IP addresses as Nmap will try to resolve the reverse DNS information of every IP address. The reverse DNS information can reveal interesting information about the target IP address (even if it is offline or blocking Nmap's probes).

> **Note** *The **-R** option can dramatically reduce the performance of a scan.*

Disable Reverse DNS Resolution

The **-n** parameter is used to disable reverse DNS lookups.

Usage syntax: nmap -n [target]

```
# nmap -n 64.13.134.52

Starting Nmap 5.00 ( http://nmap.org ) at 2009-08-13 17:23 Central
Daylight Time

Interesting ports on 64.13.134.52:
Not shown: 993 filtered ports
PORT        STATE   SERVICE
25/tcp      closed  smtp
53/tcp      open    domain
70/tcp      closed  gopher
80/tcp      open    http
110/tcp     closed  pop3
113/tcp     closed  auth
31337/tcp   closed  Elite

Nmap done: 1 IP address (1 host up) scanned in 8.48 seconds
```

Output of a Nmap scan with reverse DNS disabled

Reverse DNS dramatically can significantly slow an Nmap scan. Using the **-n** option greatly reduces scanning times - especially when scanning a large number of hosts. This option is useful if you don't care about the DNS information for the target system and prefer to perform a scan which produces faster results.

Alternative DNS Lookup Method

The **--system-dns** option instructs Nmap to use the host system's DNS resolver instead of its own internal method.

Usage syntax: nmap --system-dns [target]

```
$ nmap --system-dns scanme.insecure.org

Starting Nmap 5.00 ( http://nmap.org ) at 2009-08-09 21:47 CDT
Interesting ports on scanme.nmap.org (64.13.134.52):
Not shown: 972 closed ports, 26 filtered ports
PORT    STATE SERVICE
53/tcp  open  domain
80/tcp  open  http

Nmap done: 1 IP address (1 host up) scanned in 19.86 second
```

Output of a Nmap scan using the system DNS resolver

This option is rarely used as it is much slower than the default method. It can, however, be useful when troubleshooting DNS problems with Nmap.

> **Note** *The system resolver is always used for IPv6 scans as Nmap has not yet fully implemented its own internal IPv6 resolver.*

Manually Specify DNS Server(s)

The **--dns-servers** option is used to manually specify DNS servers to be queried when scanning.

Usage syntax: nmap --dns-servers [server1,server2,etc] [target]

```
$ nmap --dns-servers 208.67.222.222,208.67.220.220 scanme.insecure.org

Starting Nmap 5.00 ( http://nmap.org ) at 2009-08-09 22:40 CDT
Interesting ports on scanme.nmap.org (64.13.134.52):
Not shown: 998 closed ports
PORT     STATE SERVICE
53/tcp   open  domain
80/tcp   open  http

Nmap done: 1 IP address (1 host up) scanned in 32.07 seconds
```

Manually specifying DNS servers

Nmap's default behavior will use the DNS servers configured on your local system for name resolution. The **--dns-servers** option allows you to specify one or more alternative servers for Nmap to query. This can be useful for systems that do not have DNS configured or if you want to prevent your scan lookups from appearing in your locally configured DNS server's log file.

> **Note** *This option is currently not available for IPv6 scans.*

Create a Host List

The **-sL** option will display a list and performs a reverse DNS lookup of the specified IP addresses.

Usage syntax: nmap -sL [target]

```
$ nmap -sL 10.10.1.1/24

Starting Nmap 5.00 ( http://nmap.org ) at 2009-08-14 13:56 CDT
Host 10.10.1.0 not scanned
Host router.nmapcookbook.com (10.10.1.1) not scanned
Host server.nmapcookbook.com (10.10.1.2) not scanned
Host 10.10.1.3 not scanned
Host 10.10.1.4 not scanned
Host mylaptop.nmapcookbook.com (10.10.1.5) not scanned
Host 10.10.1.6 not scanned
Host 10.10.1.7 not scanned
Host 10.10.1.8 not scanned
Host mydesktop.nmapcookbook.com (10.10.1.9) not scanned
Host mydesktop2.nmapcookbook.com (10.10.1.10) not scanned
Host 10.10.1.11 not scanned
Host 10.10.1.12 not scanned
Host 10.10.1.13 not scanned
Host 10.10.1.14 not scanned
Host 10.10.1.15 not scanned
Host 10.10.1.16 not scanned
Host 10.10.1.17 not scanned
...
```

Output of a host list generated by Nmap

The above scan shows the results of the DNS names for the specified systems. This scan is useful for identifying the IP addresses and DNS names for the specified targets without sending any packets to them. Many DNS names can reveal interesting information about an IP address including what it used for or where it is located.

Section 4:
Advanced Scanning Options

Advanced Scanning Functions Overview

Nmap supports a number of user selectable scan types. By default, Nmap will perform a basic TCP scan on each target system. In some situations, it may be necessary to perform more complex TCP (or even UDP) scans in an attempt to find uncommon services or to evade a firewall. These advanced scan types are covered in this section.

Summary of features covered in this section:

Feature	Option
TCP SYN Scan	-sS
TCP Connect Scan	-sT
UDP Scan	-sU
TCP NULL Scan	-sN
TCP FIN Scan	-sF
Xmas Scan	-sX
TCP ACK Scan	-sA
Custom TCP Scan	--scanflags
IP Protocol Scan	-sO
Send Raw Ethernet Packets	--send-eth
Send IP Packets	--send-ip

Note: *You must login with root/administrator privileges (or use the **sudo** command) to execute many of the scans discussed in this section.*

TCP SYN Scan

The **-sS** option performs a TCP SYN scan.

Usage syntax: nmap -sS [target]

```
# nmap -sS 10.10.1.48

Starting Nmap 5.00 ( http://nmap.org ) at 2009-08-25 11:01 CDT
Interesting ports on 10.10.1.48:
Not shown: 994 closed ports
PORT       STATE  SERVICE
21/tcp     open   ftp
22/tcp     open   ssh
25/tcp     open   smtp
80/tcp     open   http
111/tcp    open   rpcbind
2049/tcp   open   nfs
MAC Address: 00:0C:29:D5:38:F4 (VMware)

Nmap done: 1 IP address (1 host up) scanned in 1.73 seconds
```

Performing a TCP SYN scan

The TCP SYN scan is the default option for privileged users (users running as root on Unix/Linux or Administrator on Windows). The default TCP SYN scan attempts to identify the 1000 most commonly used TCP ports by sending a SYN packet to the target and listening for a response. This type of scan is said to be stealthy because it does not attempt to open a full-fledged connection to the remote host. This prevents many systems from logging a connection attempt from your scan.

> **Note**
> *Stealth operation is not guaranteed. Modern packet capture programs and advanced firewalls are now able to detect TCP SYN scans.*

TCP Connect Scan

The **-sT** option performs a TCP connect scan.

Usage syntax: nmap -sT [target]

```
$ nmap -sT 10.10.1.1

Starting Nmap 5.00 ( http://nmap.org ) at 2009-08-31 13:06 CDT
Interesting ports on 10.10.1.1:
Not shown: 998 closed ports
PORT     STATE SERVICE
80/tcp   open  http
443/tcp  open  https

Nmap done: 1 IP address (1 host up) scanned in 0.56 seconds
```

Performing a TCP connect scan

The **-sT** scan is the default scan type for non-privileged users. It is also used when scanning IPv6 targets. The TCP Connect Scan is a simple probe that attempts to directly connect to the remote system without using any stealth (as described on page 67).

> **Tip**: *It is typically best to execute Nmap with root privileges whenever possible as it will perform a TCP SYN scan (-sS) which can provide a more accurate listing of port states and is significantly faster.*

UDP Scan

The **-sU** option performs a UDP (User Datagram Protocol) scan.

Usage syntax: nmap -sU [target]

```
# nmap -sU 10.10.1.41

Starting Nmap 5.00 ( http://nmap.org ) at 2009-09-06 21:20 CDT
Interesting ports on 10.10.1.41:
Not shown: 984 closed ports
PORT       STATE           SERVICE
7/udp      open            echo
9/udp      open|filtered   discard
13/udp     open            daytime
19/udp     open            chargen
37/udp     open            time
69/udp     open|filtered   tftp
111/udp    open|filtered   rpcbind
137/udp    open|filtered   netbios-ns
138/udp    open|filtered   netbios-dgm
177/udp    open|filtered   xdmcp
514/udp    open|filtered   syslog
518/udp    open|filtered   ntalk
1028/udp   open|filtered   ms-lsa
1030/udp   open|filtered   iad1
2049/udp   open|filtered   nfs
MAC Address: 00:60:B0:59:B6:14 (Hewlett-packard CO.)

Nmap done: 1 IP address (1 host up) scanned in 1.91 seconds
```

Performing a UDP scan

The example above displays the results of a UDP scan. While TCP is the most commonly used protocol, many network services (like DNS, DHCP, and SNMP) still utilize UDP. When performing a network audit, it's always a good idea to check for both TCP *and* UDP services to get a more complete picture of the target host/network.

NULL Scan

The **-sN** option performs a TCP NULL scan.

Usage syntax: nmap -sN [target]

```
# nmap -sN 10.10.1.48

Starting Nmap 5.00 ( http://nmap.org ) at 2009-10-01 13:19 CDT
Interesting ports on 10.10.1.48:
Not shown: 994 closed ports
PORT       STATE           SERVICE
21/tcp     open|filtered   ftp
22/tcp     open|filtered   ssh
25/tcp     open|filtered   smtp
80/tcp     open|filtered   http
111/tcp    open|filtered   rpcbind
2049/tcp   open|filtered   nfs
MAC Address: 00:0C:29:D5:38:F4 (VMware)

Nmap done: 1 IP address (1 host up) scanned in 1.54 seconds
```
Performing a TCP NULL scan

A TCP NULL scan causes Nmap to send packets with no TCP flags enabled. This is done by setting the packet header to 0. Sending NULL packets to a target is a method of tricking a firewalled system to generate a response.

> **Note** *Not all systems will respond to probes of this type.*

See also: --scanflags (page 73)

TCP FIN Scan

The **-sF** option performs a TCP FIN scan.

Usage syntax: nmap -sF [target]

```
# nmap -sF 10.10.1.48

Starting Nmap 5.00 ( http://nmap.org ) at 2009-10-01 13:21 CDT
Interesting ports on 10.10.1.48:
Not shown: 994 closed ports
PORT       STATE          SERVICE
21/tcp     open|filtered  ftp
22/tcp     open|filtered  ssh
25/tcp     open|filtered  smtp
80/tcp     open|filtered  http
111/tcp    open|filtered  rpcbind
2049/tcp   open|filtered  nfs
MAC Address: 00:0C:29:D5:38:F4 (VMware)

Nmap done: 1 IP address (1 host up) scanned in 1.59 seconds
```

Performing a TCP FIN scan

In a **-sF** scan, Nmap marks the TCP FIN bit active when sending packets in an attempt to solicit a TCP ACK from the specified target system. This is another method of sending unexpected packets to a target in an attempt to produce results from a system protected by a firewall.

> **Note** *Not all systems will respond to probes of this type.*

See also: --scanflags (page 73)

Xmas Scan

The **-sX** flag performs a Xmas scan.

Usage syntax: nmap -sX [target]

```
# nmap -sX 10.10.1.48

Starting Nmap 5.00 ( http://nmap.org ) at 2009-10-01 13:34 CDT
Interesting ports on 10.10.1.48:
Not shown: 994 closed ports
PORT       STATE             SERVICE
21/tcp     open|filtered     ftp
22/tcp     open|filtered     ssh
25/tcp     open|filtered     smtp
80/tcp     open|filtered     http
111/tcp    open|filtered     rpcbind
2049/tcp   open|filtered     nfs
MAC Address: 00:0C:29:D5:38:F4 (VMware)

Nmap done: 1 IP address (1 host up) scanned in 2.89 seconds
```

Performing a "Christmas" scan

In the Xmas scan, Nmap sends packets with URG, FIN, and PSH, and flags activated. This has the effect of "lighting the packet up like a Christmas tree" and can occasionally solicit a response from a firewalled system.

> **Note** *Not all systems will respond to probes of this type.*

See also: --scanflags (page 73)

Custom TCP Scan

The **--scanflags** option is used perform a custom TCP scan.

Usage syntax: nmap --scanflags [flag(s)] [target]

```
# nmap --scanflags SYNURG 10.10.1.127

Starting Nmap 5.00 ( http://nmap.org ) at 2009-11-12 14:53 CST
Interesting ports on 10.10.1.127:
Not shown: 996 filtered ports
PORT       STATE   SERVICE
139/tcp    open    netbios-ssn
445/tcp    open    microsoft-ds
3389/tcp   closed  ms-term-serv
5900/tcp   open    vnc
MAC Address: 00:14:22:59:3D:DE (Dell)

Nmap done: 1 IP address (1 host up) scanned in 4.67 seconds
```

Manually specifying TCP flags

The **--scanflags** option allows users to define a custom scan using one or more TCP header flags. Any combination of flags listed in the table below can be used with the **--scanflags** option. For example: **nmap --scanflags FINACK** (no space) would activate the FIN and ACK TCP flags.

Flag	Usage
SYN	Synchronize
ACK	Acknowledgment
PSH	Push
URG	Urgent
RST	Reset
FIN	Finished

TCP header flags

TCP ACK Scan

The **-sA** option performs a TCP ACK scan.

Usage syntax: nmap -sA [target]

```
# nmap -sA 10.10.1.70

Starting Nmap 5.00 ( http://nmap.org ) at 2009-12-18 10:33 CST
Interesting ports on 10.10.1.70:
Not shown: 994 filtered ports
PORT        STATE       SERVICE
139/tcp     unfiltered  netbios-ssn
445/tcp     unfiltered  microsoft-ds
2967/tcp    unfiltered  symantec-av
5900/tcp    unfiltered  vnc
19283/tcp   unfiltered  unknown
19315/tcp   unfiltered  unknown
MAC Address: 00:0C:F1:A6:1F:16 (Intel)

Nmap done: 1 IP address (1 host up) scanned in 5.33 seconds
```

Performing a TCP ACK scan

The **-sA** option can be used to determine if the target system is protected by a firewall. When performing a TCP ACK scan, Nmap will probe a target and look for RST responses. If no response is received the system is considered to be filtered. If the system does return an RST packet, then it is labeled as unfiltered. In the above example 994 ports are labeled as filtered meaning that the system is likely protected by a firewall. The 6 unfiltered ports displayed are likely to have special rules in the target's firewall that enable them to be open or closed.

> **Note**
>
> The **-sA** option does not display whether or not the unfiltered ports are open or closed. Its only purpose is to determine whether or not the system is filtering ports.

IP Protocol Scan

The **-sO** option performs an IP protocol scan.

Usage syntax: nmap -sO [target]

```
# nmap -sO 10.10.1.41

Starting Nmap 5.00 ( http://nmap.org ) at 2009-09-06 21:32 CDT
Interesting protocols on 10.10.1.41:
Not shown: 253 open|filtered protocols
PROTOCOL STATE SERVICE
1        open  icmp
6        open  tcp
17       open  udp
MAC Address: 00:60:B0:59:B6:14 (Hewlett-packard CO.)

Nmap done: 1 IP address (1 host up) scanned in 2.81 seconds
```

Output of a IP protocol scan

The IP protocol scan displays the IP protocols that are supported on the target system. The most commonly found protocols on modern networks are ICMP, TCP, and UDP as displayed in the above example. Using the **-sO** option is helpful for quickly identifying what types of scans you want to perform on the selected target system based on its supported protocols.

> **Tip:** *A complete list of IP protocols can be found on the IANA website at www.iana.org/assignments/protocol-numbers/.*

Send Raw Ethernet Packets

The **--send-eth** option instructs Nmap to use raw ethernet packets while scanning.

Usage syntax: nmap --send-eth [target]

```
$ nmap --send-eth 10.10.1.51

Starting Nmap 5.00 ( http://nmap.org ) at 2009-10-01 14:19 CDT
Interesting ports on 10.10.1.51:
Not shown: 997 closed ports
PORT        STATE  SERVICE
80/tcp      open   http
443/tcp     open   https
49152/tcp   open   unknown

Nmap done: 1 IP address (1 host up) scanned in 0.22 seconds
```

Scan using raw ethernet packets

Enabling this option instructs Nmap to bypass the IP layer on your system and send raw ethernet packets on the data link layer. This can be used to overcome problems with your system's IP stack.

> **Note**
> The **--send-eth** option is automatically implied by Nmap where needed so it is rarely used as a command line argument.

See also: --send-ip (page 77)

Send IP Packets

The **--send-ip** option instructs Nmap to use IP packets while scanning.

Usage syntax: nmap --send-ip [target]

```
$ nmap --send-ip 10.10.1.51

Starting Nmap 5.00 ( http://nmap.org ) at 2009-10-01 14:15 CDT
Interesting ports on 10.10.1.51:
Not shown: 997 closed ports
PORT       STATE SERVICE
80/tcp     open  http
443/tcp    open  https
49152/tcp  open  unknown

Nmap done: 1 IP address (1 host up) scanned in 0.19 seconds
```
Scan using IP packets

Enabling this option forces Nmap to scan using the local system's IP stack instead of generating raw ethernet packets.

> **Note**
> The **--send-ip** option is automatically implied by Nmap where needed so it is rarely used as a command line argument.

See also: --send-eth (page 76)

77

Section 5:

Port Scanning Options

Port Scanning Options Overview

There are a total of 131,070 TCP/IP ports (65,535 TCP and 65,535 UDP). Nmap, by default, only scans 1,000 of the most commonly used ports. This is done to save time when scanning multiple targets as the majority of ports outside the top 1000 are rarely used. Sometimes, however, you may want to scan outside the default range of ports to look for uncommon services or ports that have been forwarded to a different location. This section covers the options which allow this and other port specific features.

> **Tip**
> *A complete list of TCP/IP ports can be found on the IANA website at www.iana.org/assignments/port-numbers.*

Summary of features covered in this section:

Feature	Option
Perform a Fast Scan	-F
Scan Specific Ports	-p [port]
Scan Ports by Name	-p [name]
Scan Ports by Protocol	-p U:[UDP ports],T:[TCP ports]
Scan All Ports	-p "*"
Scan Top Ports	--top-ports [number]
Perform a Sequential Port Scan	-r

Perform a Fast Scan

The **-F** option instructs Nmap to perform a scan of only the 100 most commonly used ports.

Usage syntax: nmap -F [target]

```
$ nmap -F 10.10.1.44

Starting Nmap 5.00 ( http://nmap.org ) at 2009-08-13 10:13 CDT
Interesting ports on 10.10.1.44:
Not shown: 91 closed ports
PORT       STATE SERVICE
25/tcp     open  smtp
53/tcp     open  domain
80/tcp     open  http
135/tcp    open  msrpc
139/tcp    open  netbios-ssn
445/tcp    open  microsoft-ds
3389/tcp   open  ms-term-serv
8000/tcp   open  http-alt
10000/tcp  open  snet-sensor-mgmt

Nmap done: 1 IP address (1 host up) scanned in 2.43 seconds
```
Output of a "fast" scan

Nmap scans the top 1000 commonly used ports by default. The **-F** option reduces that number to 100. This can dramatically speed up scanning while still representing the majority of commonly used ports.

Scan Specific Ports

The **-p** option is used to instruct Nmap to scan the specified port(s).

Usage syntax: nmap -p [port] [target]

```
$ nmap -p 80 10.10.1.44

Starting Nmap 5.00 ( http://nmap.org ) at 2009-08-13 10:10 CDT
Interesting ports on 10.10.1.44:
PORT    STATE SERVICE
80/tcp  open  http

Nmap done: 1 IP address (1 host up) scanned in 0.12 seconds
```
Specifying a single port to scan

The example above demonstrates using **-p** to scan port 80. In addition to scanning a single port, you can scan multiple individual ports (separated by a comma) or a range of ports as demonstrated in the next example.

Usage syntax: nmap [port1,port2,etc|range of ports] [target]

```
$ nmap -p 25,53,80-200 10.10.1.44

Starting Nmap 5.00 ( http://nmap.org ) at 2009-08-13 10:10 CDT
Interesting ports on 10.10.1.44:
Not shown: 118 closed ports
PORT     STATE SERVICE
25/tcp   open  smtp
53/tcp   open  domain
80/tcp   open  http
135/tcp  open  msrpc
139/tcp  open  netbios-ssn

Nmap done: 1 IP address (1 host up) scanned in 0.15 seconds
```
Specifying multiple ports to scan

In this example the **-p** option is used to scan ports 25, 53, and 80 through 200.

Scan Ports by Name

The **-p** option can be used to scan ports by name.

Usage syntax: nmap -p [port name(s)] [target]

```
$ nmap -p smtp,http 10.10.1.44

Starting Nmap 5.00 ( http://nmap.org ) at 2009-08-17 10:37 CDT
Interesting ports on 10.10.1.44:
PORT       STATE   SERVICE
25/tcp     open    smtp
80/tcp     open    http
8008/tcp   closed  http

Nmap done: 1 IP address (1 host up) scanned in 0.10 seconds
```

Scanning ports by name

The example above demonstrates searching for open SMTP and HTTP ports by name using the **-p** option. The name(s) specified must match a service in the nmap-services file. This is usually found in **/usr/local/share/nmap/** on Unix/Linux systems or **C:\Program Files\Nmap** on Windows systems.

Wildcards can also be used when specifying services by name. For example, executing **nmap -p "http*" 10.10.1.44** would scan for all ports that start with http (including http and https).

> **Note** *You must enclose the wildcard statement in quotes so your system does not interpret it as a shell wildcard.*

Scan Ports by Protocol

Specifying a T: or U: prefix with the **-p** option allows you to search for a specific port and protocol combination.

Usage syntax: nmap -p U:[UDP ports],T:[TCP ports] [target]

```
# nmap -sU -sT -p U:53,T:25 10.10.1.44

Starting Nmap 5.00 ( http://nmap.org ) at 2009-08-18 12:52 CDT
Interesting ports on 10.10.1.44:
PORT    STATE SERVICE
25/tcp  open  smtp
53/udp  open  domain
MAC Address: 00:14:22:0F:3C:0E (Dell)

Nmap done: 1 IP address (1 host up) scanned in 0.19 seconds
```

Scanning specific ports by protocol

Using the syntax **-p U:53,T:25** instructs Nmap to perform a UDP scan on port 53 and a TCP scan on port 25.

> **Note**
> *Nmap, by default, will only scan TCP ports. In order to scan both TCP and UDP ports you will need to enable additional scan types such as -sU and -sT which are covered in Section 4 of this book.*

Scan All Ports

The **-p "*"** option is a wildcard used to scan all 65,535 TCP/IP ports on the specified target.

Usage syntax: nmap -p "*" [target]

```
# nmap -p "*" 10.10.1.41

Starting Nmap 5.00 ( http://nmap.org ) at 2009-12-16 14:07 Central
Standard Time

Interesting ports on 10.10.1.41:
Not shown: 4204 closed ports
PORT       STATE      SERVICE
7/tcp      open       echo
9/tcp      open       discard
13/tcp     open       daytime
19/tcp     open       chargen
21/tcp     open       ftp
23/tcp     open       telnet
25/tcp     open       smtp
37/tcp     open       time
111/tcp    open       rpcbind
113/tcp    open       auth
139/tcp    open       netbios-ssn
512/tcp    open       exec
513/tcp    open       login
514/tcp    open       shell
515/tcp    open       printer
543/tcp    open       klogin
...
```

Scanning all ports on a target system

> **Note**
> You must enclose the wildcard statement in quotes so your system does not interpret it as a shell wildcard.

85

Scan Top Ports

The **--top-ports** option is used to scan the specified number of top ranked ports.

Usage syntax: nmap --top-ports [number] [target]

```
# nmap --top-ports 10 10.10.1.41

Starting Nmap 5.00 ( http://nmap.org ) at 2009-12-15 13:46 CST
Interesting ports on 10.10.1.41:
PORT      STATE  SERVICE
21/tcp    open   ftp
22/tcp    closed ssh
23/tcp    open   telnet
25/tcp    open   smtp
80/tcp    closed http
110/tcp   closed pop3
139/tcp   open   netbios-ssn
443/tcp   closed https
445/tcp   closed microsoft-ds
3389/tcp  closed ms-term-serv
MAC Address: 00:60:B0:59:B6:14 (Hewlett-packard CO.)

Nmap done: 1 IP address (1 host up) scanned in 0.22 seconds
```

Performing a top port scan on the ten highest ranked ports

By default, Nmap will scan the 1000 most commonly used ports. The **-F** option (see page 81) reduces that number to 100. Using the **--top-ports** option, you can specify any number of top ranked ports to scan.

The example above demonstrates using the **--top-ports** option to scan the top 10 ports; however, any number can be used. For example: **nmap --top-ports 500** would scan the top 500 most commonly used ports and **nmap --top-ports 5000** would scan the top 5000 most commonly used ports.

Perform a Sequential Port Scan

The **-r** option performs a sequential port scan on the specified target.

Usage syntax: nmap -r [target]

```
$ nmap -r 10.10.1.48

Starting Nmap 5.00 ( http://nmap.org ) at 2009-08-13 13:02 CDT
Interesting ports on 10.10.1.48:
Not shown: 994 closed ports
PORT       STATE  SERVICE
21/tcp     open   ftp
22/tcp     open   ssh
25/tcp     open   smtp
80/tcp     open   http
111/tcp    open   rpcbind
2049/tcp   open   nfs

Nmap done: 1 IP address (1 host up) scanned in 0.49 seconds
```

Performing a sequentially ordered port scan

Nmap's default scanning algorithm randomizes the port scan order. This is useful for evading firewalls and intrusion prevention systems. The **-r** parameter overrides this functionality and instructs Nmap to sequentially search for open ports in numerical order.

> **Note**: The results of the **-r** scan aren't entirely evident because Nmap always sorts the final output of each scan. Combining the **-v** option with **-r** will display the sequential port discovery in real time.

Section 6:
Operating System and Service Detection

Version Detection Overview

One of Nmap's most remarkable (and incredibly useful) features is its ability to detect operating systems and services on remote systems. This feature analyzes responses from scanned targets and attempts to identify the host's operating system and installed services.

The process of identifying a target's operating system and software versions is known as TCP/IP fingerprinting. Although it is not an exact science, Nmap developers have taken great care in making TCP/IP fingerprinting an accurate and reliable feature. And, like most of Nmap's features, version detection can be controlled using an array of arguments which are covered in this section.

Summary of features covered in this section:

Feature	Option
Operating System Detection	-O
Attempt to Guess an Unknown OS	--osscan-guess
Service Version Detection	-sV
Perform a RPC Scan	--version-trace
Troubleshooting Version Scans	-sR

Operating System Detection

The **-O** parameter enables Nmap's operating system detection feature.

Usage syntax: nmap -O [target]

```
# nmap -O 10.10.1.48

Starting Nmap 5.00 ( http://nmap.org ) at 2009-08-11 13:09 Central
Daylight Time
...

MAC Address: 00:0C:29:D5:38:F4 (VMware)
Device type: general purpose
Running: Linux 2.6.X
OS details: Linux 2.6.9 - 2.6.28
Network Distance: 1 hop

...
```

Output of Nmap's operating system detection feature

As demonstrated above, Nmap is (in most cases) able to identify the operating system on a remote target. Operating system detection is performed by analyzing responses from the target for a set of predictable characteristics which can be used to identify the type of OS on the remote system.

In order for OS detection to work properly there must be at least one open and one closed port on the target system. When scanning multiple targets, the **--osscan-limit** option can be combined with **-O** to instruct Nmap not to OS scan hosts that do not meet this criteria.

> **Tip**
> The **-v** option can be combined with **-O** to display additional information Nmap discovers about the remote system.

Submitting TCP/IP Fingerprints

If Nmap is unable to determine the operating system on a target, it will provide a fingerprint which can be submitted to Nmap's OS database at www.nmap.org/submit/. The example below demonstrates Nmap's output in this scenario.

```
# nmap -O 10.10.1.11

Starting Nmap 5.00 ( http://nmap.org ) at 2009-12-16 14:16 Central
Standard Time
...
No exact OS matches for host (If you know what OS is running on it,
see http://nmap.org/submit/ ).
TCP/IP fingerprint:
OS:SCAN(V=5.00%D=12/16%OT=3001%CT=1%CU=32781%PV=Y%DS=1%G=Y%M=00204A%TM=4B29
OS:4048%P=i686-pc-windows-windows)SEQ(CI=I%II=I%TS=U)OPS(O1=M400%O2=%O3=%O4
OS:=%O5=%O6=)OPS(O1=M400%O2=M400%O3=%O4=%O5=%O6=)OPS(O1=%O2=M400%O3=M400%O4
OS:=%O5=%O6=)OPS(O1=%O2=%O3=M400%O4=%O5=%O6=)OPS(O1=M400%O2=%O3=M400%O4=%O5
OS:=%O6=)WIN(W1=7FF%W2=0%W3=0%W4=0%W5=0%W6=0)WIN(W1=7FF%W2=7FF%W3=0%W4=0%W5
OS:=0%W6=0)WIN(W1=0%W2=7FF%W3=7FF%W4=0%W5=0%W6=0)WIN(W1=0%W2=0%W3=7FF%W4=0%
OS:W5=0%W6=0)WIN(W1=7FF%W2=0%W3=7FF%W4=0%W5=0%W6=0)ECN(R=Y%DF=Y%T=40%W=0%O=
OS:%CC=N%Q=)T1(R=Y%DF=Y%T=40%S=O%A=S+%F=AS%RD=0%Q=)T1(R=Y%DF=Y%T=40%S=O%A=O
OS:%F=AS%RD=0%Q=)T1(R=Y%DF=Y%T=40%S=Z%A=S+%F=AR%RD=0%Q=)T2(R=Y%DF=Y%T=40%W=
OS:0%S=Z%A=S+%F=AR%O=%RD=0%Q=)T3(R=Y%DF=Y%T=40%W=0%S=Z%A=S+%F=AR%O=%RD=0%Q=
OS:)T4(R=Y%DF=Y%T=40%W=0%S=A%A=Z%F=R%O=%RD=0%Q=)T5(R=Y%DF=Y%T=40%W=0%S=Z%A=
OS:S+%F=AR%O=%RD=0%Q=)T6(R=Y%DF=Y%T=40%W=0%S=A%A=Z%F=R%O=%RD=0%Q=)T7(R=Y%DF
OS:=Y%T=40%W=0%S=Z%A=S+%F=AR%O=%RD=0%Q=)U1(R=Y%DF=Y%T=40%IPL=38%UN=0%RIPL=G
OS:%RID=G%RIPCK=G%RUCK=G%RUD=G)IE(R=Y%DFI=S%T=40%CD=S)
...
```

TCP/IP fingerprint generated by Nmap

By submitting the fingerprint generated and correctly identifying the target system's operating system, you can help improve the accuracy of Nmap's OS detection feature in future releases.

Attempt to Guess an Unknown Operating System

If Nmap is unable to accurately identify the OS, you can force it to guess by using the **--osscan-guess** option.

Usage syntax: nmap -O --osscan-guess [target]

```
# nmap -O --osscan-guess 10.10.1.11

Starting Nmap 5.00 ( http://nmap.org ) at 2009-08-17 13:25 CDT
Interesting ports on 10.10.1.11:
Not shown: 999 closed ports
PORT      STATE SERVICE
3001/tcp  open  nessus
MAC Address: 00:20:4A:69:FD:94 (Pronet Gmbh)
Aggressive OS guesses: Enerdis Enerium 200 energy monitoring device or
Mitsubishi XD1000 projector (96%), Lantronix UDS200 external serial
device server (96%), Lantronix Xport-03 embedded serial device server
(firmware 6.1.0.3) (95%), Larus 54580 NTP server (95%), Lantronix
Evolution OS (93%), Lantronix UDS1100 external serial device server
(92%), Lantronix XPort embedded Ethernet device server (90%),
Stonewater Control Systems environmental monitoring appliance (88%),
FreeBSD 6.3-PRERELEASE (88%), Crestron MC2E, MP2E, PRO2, or QM-RMC
control and automation system (2-Series) (87%)
...
```
Nmap operating system guess output

The example above displays a list of possible matches for the target's operating system. Each guess is listed with a percentage of confidence Nmap has in the supplied match.

> **Tip**
> The **--fuzzy** option is a synonym that can be used as an easy to remember shortcut for the **--osscan-guess** feature.

Service Version Detection

The **-sV** parameter enables Nmap's service version detection feature.

Usage syntax: nmap -sV [target]

```
# nmap -sV 10.10.1.48

Starting Nmap 5.00 ( http://nmap.org ) at 2009-08-11 12:49 Central
Daylight Time

Interesting ports on 10.10.1.48:
Not shown: 996 closed ports
PORT     STATE SERVICE VERSION
21/tcp   open  ftp     vsftpd 2.0.6
22/tcp   open  ssh     OpenSSH 4.7p1 Debian 8ubuntu1.2 (protocol 2.0)
25/tcp   open  smtp    Postfix smtpd
80/tcp   open  http    Apache httpd 2.2.8 ((Ubuntu))
MAC Address: 00:0C:29:D5:38:F4 (VMware)
Service Info: Host:  10.10.1.48; OSs: Unix, Linux

Service detection performed. Please report any incorrect results at
http://nmap.org/submit/ .

Nmap done: 1 IP address (1 host up) scanned in 8.33 seconds
```

Output of Nmap's service version detection feature

The **-sV** option will attempt to identify the vendor and software version for any open ports it detects. The results of the above scan show the software vendor and version number for services that Nmap was successfully able to identify.

> **Note**
>
> Nmap version detection purposely skips some problematic ports (specifically 9100-9107). This can be overridden by combining the *--allports* parameter with *-sV* which instructs Nmap not to exclude any ports from version detection.

Troubleshooting Version Scans

The **--version-trace** option can be enabled to display verbose version scan activity.

Usage syntax: nmap -sV --version-trace [target]

```
$ nmap -sV --version-trace 10.10.1.48

Starting Nmap 5.00 ( http://nmap.org ) at 2009-08-13 13:16 CDT
PORTS: Using top 1000 ports found open (TCP:1000, UDP:0, SCTP:0)
--------------- Timing report ---------------
  hostgroups: min 1, max 100000
  rtt-timeouts: init 1000, min 100, max 10000
  max-scan-delay: TCP 1000, UDP 1000, SCTP 1000
  parallelism: min 0, max 0
  max-retries: 10, host-timeout: 0
  min-rate: 0, max-rate: 0
---------------------------------------------
NSE: Loaded 3 scripts for scanning.
Overall sending rates: 319.95 packets / s.
Increased max_successful_tryno for 10.10.1.48 to 1 (packet drop)
Overall sending rates: 756.69 packets / s.
NSOCK (1.6000s) TCP connection requested to 10.10.1.48:21 (IOD #1) EID 8
NSOCK (1.6000s) TCP connection requested to 10.10.1.48:22 (IOD #2) EID 16
NSOCK (1.6000s) TCP connection requested to 10.10.1.48:25 (IOD #3) EID 24
NSOCK (1.6000s) TCP connection requested to 10.10.1.48:80 (IOD #4) EID 32
NSOCK (1.6000s) TCP connection requested to 10.10.1.48:111 (IOD #5) EID 40
NSOCK (1.6000s) TCP connection requested to 10.10.1.48:2049 (IOD #6) EID 48
NSOCK (1.6000s) nsock_loop() started (no timeout). 6 events pending
NSOCK (1.6010s) Callback: CONNECT SUCCESS for EID 8 [10.10.1.48:21]
...
```

Version scan trace output

The **--version-trace** option can be helpful for debugging problems or to gain additional information about the target system. For more information about troubleshooting and debugging Nmap see Section 10.

Perform an RPC Scan

The **-sR** option performs a RPC (Remote Procedure Call) scan on the specified target.

Usage syntax: nmap -sR [target]

```
$ nmap -sR 10.10.1.176

Starting Nmap 5.00 ( http://nmap.org ) at 2009-08-13 14:22 Central
Daylight Time

Interesting ports on 10.10.1.176:
Not shown: 995 closed ports
PORT       STATE  SERVICE              VERSION
22/tcp     open   ssh
111/tcp    open   rpcbind (rpcbind V2) 2 (rpc #100000)
139/tcp    open   netbios-ssn
445/tcp    open   microsoft-ds
2049/tcp   open   nfs (nfs V2-4)       2-4 (rpc #100003)
MAC Address: 00:16:EA:F0:92:50 (Intel)

Nmap done: 1 IP address (1 host up) scanned in 3.01 seconds
```

Output of a RPC scan

The output of the **-sR** scan above displays information about RPC services running on the target system. RCP is most commonly associated with Unix and Linux systems specifically for the NFS (Network File System) service. In this example, NFS version 2 RPC services are detected on ports 111 and 2049.

Section 7:
Timing Options

Timing Options Overview

Many Nmap features have configurable timing options. These timing options can be used to speed up or slow down scanning operations depending on your needs. When scanning a large number of hosts on a fast network you may want to increase the number of parallel operations to get faster results. Alternatively, when scanning slow networks (or across the internet) you may want to slow down a scan to get more accurate results or to evade intrusion detection systems. This section discusses the options available for these timing features.

Summary of features covered in this section:

Feature	Option
Timing Templates	-T[0-5]
Set the Packet TTL	--ttl
Minimum # of Parallel Operations	--min-parallelism
Maximum # of Parallel Operations	--max-parallelism
Minimum Host Group Size	--min-hostgroup
Maximum Host Group Size	--max-hostgroup
Maximum RTT Timeout	--max-rtt-timeout
Initial RTT Timeout	--initial-rtt-timeout
Maximum Retries	--max-retries
Host Timeout	--host-timeout
Minimum Scan Delay	--scan-delay
Maximum Scan Delay	--max-scan-delay
Minimum Packet Rate	--min-rate
Maximum Packet Rate	--max-rate
Defeat Reset Rate Limits	--defeat-rst-ratelimit

Timing Parameters

Nmap timing parameters are accepted as milliseconds by default. You can also specify timing parameters in seconds, minutes, or hours by appending a qualifier to the time argument. The table below provides examples of time parameter usage syntax.

Parameter	Definition	Example	Meaning
(none)	Milliseconds (1/1000 of a second)	500	500 milliseconds
s	Seconds	300s	300 seconds
m	Minutes	5m	5 minutes
h	Hours	1h	1 hour

Nmap time specification parameters

Example: The **--host-timeout** option (see page 108) uses a timing parameter. To specify a five minute timeout you can use any of the following forms of time specification:

```
nmap --host-timeout 300000 10.10.5.11
nmap --host-timeout 300s 10.10.5.11
nmap --host-timeout 5m 10.10.5.11
```

Since 300000 = 300s = 5m any of the above commands will produce the same result.

Timing Templates

The **-T** parameter is used to specify a timing template for an Nmap scan.

Usage syntax: nmap -T[0-5] [target]

```
$ nmap -T4 10.10.1.1

Starting Nmap 5.00 ( http://nmap.org ) at 2009-08-12 16:59 CDT
Interesting ports on 10.10.1.1:
Not shown: 998 closed ports
PORT      STATE SERVICE
80/tcp    open  http
443/tcp   open  https

Nmap done: 1 IP address (1 host up) scanned in 0.48 seconds
```
Using a timing template

Timing templates are handy shortcuts for various timing options (discussed later in this section). There are six templates (numbered 0-5) that can be used to speed up scanning (for faster results) or to slow down scanning (to evade firewalls). The table below describes each timing template.

Template	Name	Notes
-T0	paranoid	Extremely slow
-T1	sneaky	Useful for avoiding intrusion detection systems
-T2	polite	Unlikely to interfere with the target system
-T3	normal	This is the default timing template
-T4	aggressive	Produces faster results on local networks
-T5	insane	Very fast and aggressive scan

Nmap timing templates

Minimum Number of Parallel Operations

The **--min-parallelism** option is used to specify the minimum number of parallel port scan operations Nmap should perform at any given time.

Usage syntax: nmap --min-parallelism [number] [target]

```
# nmap --min-parallelism 100 10.10.1.70

Starting Nmap 5.00 ( http://nmap.org ) at 2009-12-17 09:02 CST
Interesting ports on 10.10.1.70:
Not shown: 994 filtered ports
PORT        STATE   SERVICE
139/tcp     open    netbios-ssn
445/tcp     open    microsoft-ds
2967/tcp    closed  symantec-av
5900/tcp    open    vnc
19283/tcp   closed  unknown
19315/tcp   closed  unknown
MAC Address: 00:0C:F1:A6:1F:16 (Intel)

Nmap done: 1 IP address (1 host up) scanned in 3.43 seconds
```

Specifying the minimum number of parallel operations

Nmap automatically adjusts parallel scanning options based on network conditions. In some rare cases you may want to specify custom settings. The above example instructs Nmap to always perform at least 100 parallel operations at any given time.

> **Note**: *While manually setting the **--min-parallelism** option may increase scan performance, setting it too high may produce inaccurate results.*

Maximum Number of Parallel Operations

The **--max-parallelism** option is used to control the maximum number of parallel port scan operations Nmap will perform at any given time.

Usage syntax: nmap --max-parallelism [number] [target]

```
# nmap --max-parallelism 1 10.10.1.70

Starting Nmap 5.00 ( http://nmap.org ) at 2009-12-17 09:03 CST
Interesting ports on 10.10.1.70:
Not shown: 994 filtered ports
PORT        STATE   SERVICE
139/tcp     open    netbios-ssn
445/tcp     open    microsoft-ds
2967/tcp    closed  symantec-av
5900/tcp    open    vnc
19283/tcp   closed  unknown
19315/tcp   closed  unknown
MAC Address: 00:0C:F1:A6:1F:16 (Intel)

Nmap done: 1 IP address (1 host up) scanned in 213.76 seconds
```

Specifying the maximum number of parallel operations

In the above example **--max-parallelism 1** is used to restrict Nmap so that only one operation is performed at a time. This scan will be considerably slow, but will be less likely to overwhelm the target system with a flood of packets.

Minimum Host Group Size

The **--min-hostgroup** option is used to specify the minimum number of targets Nmap should scan in parallel.

Usage syntax: nmap --min-hostgroup [number] [targets]

```
# nmap --min-hostgroup 30 10.10.1.0/24

Starting Nmap 5.00 ( http://nmap.org ) at 2009-11-10 10:17 CST
Interesting ports on 10.10.1.1:
Not shown: 998 closed ports
PORT     STATE SERVICE
80/tcp   open  http
443/tcp  open  https
MAC Address: 00:06:B1:12:0D:14 (Sonicwall)

Interesting ports on 10.10.1.2:
Not shown: 998 closed ports
PORT     STATE SERVICE
23/tcp   open  telnet
80/tcp   open  http
MAC Address: 00:19:B9:A6:ED:D9 (Dell)
...
```

Specifying a minimum host group size

Nmap will perform scans in parallel to save time when scanning multiple targets such as a range or entire subnet. By default, Nmap will automatically adjust the size of the host groups based on the type of scan being performed and network conditions. By specifying the **--min-hostgroup** option, Nmap will attempt to keep the group sizes above the specified number.

Maximum Host Group Size

The **--max-hostgroup** option is used to specify the maximum number of targets Nmap should scan in parallel.

Usage syntax: nmap --max-hostgroup [number] [targets]

```
# nmap --max-hostgroup 10 10.10.1.0/24

Starting Nmap 5.00 ( http://nmap.org ) at 2009-11-10 10:18 CST
Interesting ports on 10.10.1.1:
Not shown: 998 closed ports
PORT     STATE SERVICE
80/tcp   open  http
443/tcp  open  https
MAC Address: 00:06:B1:12:0D:14 (Sonicwall)

Interesting ports on 10.10.1.2:
Not shown: 998 closed ports
PORT     STATE SERVICE
23/tcp   open  telnet
80/tcp   open  http
MAC Address: 00:19:B9:A6:ED:D9 (Dell)
...
```

Specifying a maximum host group size

In contrast to the **--min-hostgroup** option, the **--max-hostgroup** option controls the maximum number of hosts in a group. This option is helpful if you want to reduce the load on a network or to avoid triggering any red flags with various network security products.

Initial RTT Timeout

The **--initial-rtt-timeout** option controls the initial RTT (round-trip time) timeout value used by Nmap.

Usage syntax: nmap --initial-rtt-timeout [time] [target]

```
# nmap --initial-rtt-timeout 5000 scanme.insecure.org

Starting Nmap 5.00 ( http://nmap.org ) at 2009-12-16 16:23 CST
Interesting ports on scanme.nmap.org (64.13.134.52):
Not shown: 998 filtered ports
PORT        STATE   SERVICE
53/tcp      open    domain
80/tcp      open    http

Nmap done: 1 IP address (1 host up) scanned in 8.31 seconds
```

Specifying the initial RTT timeout value used by Nmap

The default timing template (-T3; see page 100) has an **--initial-rtt-timeout** value of 1000 milliseconds. Increasing the value will reduce the number of packet retransmissions due to timeouts. By decreasing the value you can speed up scans; but do so with caution. Setting the RTT timeout value too low can negate any potential performance gains and lead to inaccurate results.

Maximum RTT Timeout

The **--max-rtt-timeout** option is used to specify the maximum RTT (Round-Trip Time) timeout for a packet response.

Usage syntax: `nmap --max-rtt-timeout [time] [target]`

```
# nmap --max-rtt-timeout 400 scanme.insecure.org

Starting Nmap 5.00 ( http://nmap.org ) at 2009-11-14 12:57 CST
Interesting ports on scanme.nmap.org (64.13.134.52):
Not shown: 993 filtered ports
PORT        STATE   SERVICE
25/tcp      closed  smtp
53/tcp      open    domain
70/tcp      closed  gopher
80/tcp      open    http
110/tcp     closed  pop3
113/tcp     closed  auth
31337/tcp   closed  Elite

Nmap done: 1 IP address (1 host up) scanned in 8.11 seconds
```

Specifying a 400 millisecond maximum RTT timeout

Nmap dynamically adjusts RTT timeout options for best results by default. The default maximum RTT timeout is 10 seconds. Manually adjusting the maximum RTT timeout lower will allow for faster scan times (especially when scanning large blocks of addresses). Specifying a high maximum RTT timeout will prevent Nmap from giving up too soon when scanning over slow/unreliable connections. Typical values are between 100 milliseconds for fast/reliable networks and 10000 milliseconds for slow/unreliable connections.

Maximum Retries

The **--max-retries** option is used to control the maximum number of probe retransmissions Nmap will attempt to perform.

Usage syntax: nmap --max-retries [number] [target]

```
# nmap --max-retries 1 scanme.insecure.org

Starting Nmap 5.00 ( http://nmap.org ) at 2009-11-10 09:59 CST
Interesting ports on scanme.nmap.org (64.13.134.52):
Not shown: 993 filtered ports
PORT       STATE   SERVICE
25/tcp     closed  smtp
53/tcp     open    domain
70/tcp     closed  gopher
80/tcp     open    http
110/tcp    closed  pop3
113/tcp    closed  auth
31337/tcp  closed  Elite

Nmap done: 1 IP address (1 host up) scanned in 7.55 seconds
```

Specifying the maximum number of retries

By default, Nmap will automatically adjust the number of probe retransmissions based on network conditions. The **--max-retries** option can be used if you want to override the default settings or troubleshoot a connectivity problem. Specifying a high number can increase the time it takes for a scan to complete, but will produce more accurate results. By lowering the **--max-retries** you can speed up a scan – although you may not get accurate results if Nmap gives up too quickly.

Set the Packet TTL

The **--ttl** option is used to specify the TTL (time-to-live) for the specified scan (in milliseconds).

Usage syntax: nmap --ttl [time] [target]

```
# nmap --ttl 500 scanme.insecure.org

Starting Nmap 5.00 ( http://nmap.org ) at 2009-08-24 13:19 CDT
Interesting ports on scanme.nmap.org (64.13.134.52):
Not shown: 993 filtered ports
PORT       STATE  SERVICE
25/tcp     closed smtp
53/tcp     open   domain
70/tcp     closed gopher
80/tcp     open   http
110/tcp    closed pop3
113/tcp    closed auth
31337/tcp  closed Elite

Nmap done: 1 IP address (1 host up) scanned in 7.04 seconds
```

Specifying a TTL parameter of 500 milliseconds

Packets sent using this option will have the specified TTL value. This option is useful when scanning targets on slow connections where normal packets may time out before receiving a response.

Host Timeout

The **--host-timeout** option causes Nmap to give up on slow hosts after the specified time.

Usage syntax: nmap --host-timeout [time] [target]

```
# nmap --host-timeout 1m 10.10.5.11

Starting Nmap 5.00 ( http://nmap.org ) at 2009-10-09 13:29 CDT
Skipping host 10.10.5.11 due to host timeout

Nmap done: 1 IP address (1 host up) scanned in 60.19 seconds
```
Output of a Nmap scan when specifying a 1 minute timeout

A host may take a long time to scan if it is located on a slow or unreliable network. Systems that are protected by rate limiting firewalls may also take a considerable amount of time to scan. The **--host-timeout** option instructs Nmap to give up on the target system if it fails to complete after the specified time interval. In the above example, the scan takes longer than one minute to complete (as specified by the 1m parameter) which causes Nmap to terminate the scan. This option is particularly useful when scanning multiple systems across a WAN or internet connection.

Note
Nmap performs parallel operations when scanning multiple targets. In the event that one host is taking a long time to respond, Nmap is likely scanning other hosts during that time. This reduces potential bottlenecks that slow hosts can create.

Warning
*When the **--host-timeout** option is specified, Nmap will not display any results if a host exceeds the timeout (even if it discovered open ports).*

Minimum Scan Delay

The **--scan-delay** option instructs Nmap to pause for the specified time interval between probes.

Usage syntax: nmap --scan-delay [time] [target]

```
# nmap --scan-delay 5s scanme.insecure.org

Starting Nmap 5.00 ( http://nmap.org ) at 2009-11-04 13:29 CST
Interesting ports on 64.13.134.52:
Not shown: 993 filtered ports
PORT        STATE   SERVICE
25/tcp      closed  smtp
53/tcp      open    domain
70/tcp      closed  gopher
80/tcp      open    http
110/tcp     closed  pop3
113/tcp     closed  auth
31337/tcp   closed  Elite

Nmap done: 1 IP address (1 host up) scanned in 229.28 seconds
```

Specifying a 5 second minimum scan delay

Some systems employ rate limiting which can hamper Nmap scanning attempts. Nmap will automatically adjust the scan delay by default on systems where rate limiting is detected. In some cases it may be useful to specify your own scan delay if you know that rate limiting or IDS (Intrusion Detection Systems) are in use. In the example above the scan delay of **5s** instructs Nmap to wait five seconds between probes.

Maximum Scan Delay

The **--max-scan-delay** is used to specify the maximum amount of time Nmap should wait between probes.

Usage syntax: nmap --max-scan-delay [time] [target]

```
# nmap --max-scan-delay 300 scanme.insecure.org

Starting Nmap 5.00 ( http://nmap.org ) at 2009-11-09 15:35 CST
Interesting ports on scanme.nmap.org (64.13.134.52):
Not shown: 993 filtered ports
PORT        STATE   SERVICE
25/tcp      closed  smtp
53/tcp      open    domain
70/tcp      closed  gopher
80/tcp      open    http
110/tcp     closed  pop3
113/tcp     closed  auth
31337/tcp   closed  Elite

Nmap done: 1 IP address (1 host up) scanned in 8.14 seconds
```

Specifying a 30 millisecond maximum scan delay

Nmap automatically adjusts the scan delay to adjust for network conditions and/or rate limiting hosts. The **--max-scan-delay** option can be used to provide an upper limit to the amount of time between probes. This can speed up a scan, but comes at the expense of accurate results and added network stress.

Minimum Packet Rate

The **--min-rate** option is used to specify the minimum number of packets Nmap should send per second.

Usage syntax: nmap --min-rate [number] [target]

```
# nmap --min-rate 30 scanme.insecure.org

Starting Nmap 5.00 ( http://nmap.org ) at 2009-11-10 14:13 CST
Interesting ports on scanme.nmap.org (64.13.134.52):
Not shown: 993 filtered ports
PORT       STATE  SERVICE
25/tcp     closed smtp
53/tcp     open   domain
70/tcp     closed gopher
80/tcp     open   http
110/tcp    closed pop3
113/tcp    closed auth
31337/tcp  closed Elite

Nmap done: 1 IP address (1 host up) scanned in 6.99 seconds
```

Specifying a minimum packet transmission rate of 30

Nmap, by default, will automatically adjust the packet rate for a scan based on network conditions. In some cases you may want to specify your own minimum rate - although this is generally not recommended. In the above example **--min-rate 30** instructs Nmap to send at least 30 packets per a second. Nmap will use the number as a low threshold but may scan faster than this if network conditions allow.

> **Warning** *Setting the **--min-rate** too high may reduce the accuracy of a scan.*

Maximum Packet Rate

The **--max-rate** option is used to specify the maximum number of packets Nmap should send per second.

Usage syntax: `nmap --max-rate [number] [target]`

```
# nmap --max-rate 30 scanme.insecure.org

Starting Nmap 5.00 ( http://nmap.org ) at 2009-11-10 14:14 CST
Interesting ports on scanme.nmap.org (64.13.134.52):
Not shown: 993 filtered ports
PORT       STATE  SERVICE
25/tcp     closed smtp
53/tcp     open   domain
70/tcp     closed gopher
80/tcp     open   http
110/tcp    closed pop3
113/tcp    closed auth
31337/tcp  closed Elite

Nmap done: 1 IP address (1 host up) scanned in 68.51 seconds
```

Specifying a maximum packet transmission rate of 30

In the example above, specifying **--max-rate 30** instructs Nmap to send no more that 30 packets per second. This can dramatically slow down a scan but can be helpful when attempting to avoid intrusion detection systems or a target that uses rate limiting.

> **Tip**
> *To perform a very sneaky scan use **--max-rate 0.1** which instructs Nmap to send one packet every ten seconds.*

Defeat Reset Rate Limits

The **--defeat-rst-ratelimit** is used to defeat targets that apply rate limiting to RST (reset) packets.

Usage syntax: `nmap --defeat-rst-ratelimit [target]`

```
# nmap --defeat-rst-ratelimit scanme.insecure.org

Starting Nmap 5.00 ( http://nmap.org ) at 2009-11-10 15:14 CST
Interesting ports on scanme.nmap.org (64.13.134.52):
Not shown: 993 filtered ports
PORT        STATE  SERVICE
25/tcp      closed smtp
53/tcp      open   domain
70/tcp      closed gopher
80/tcp      open   http
110/tcp     closed pop3
113/tcp     closed auth
31337/tcp   closed Elite

Nmap done: 1 IP address (1 host up) scanned in 7.71 seconds
```

Defeating RST rate limits

The **--defeat-rst-ratelimit** option can be useful if you want to speed up scans on targets that implement RST packet rate limits. It can, however, lead to inaccurate results and as such it is rarely used.

> **Note**
> The **--defeat-rst-ratelimit** option is rarely used because, in most cases, Nmap will automatically detect rate limiting hosts and adjust itself accordingly.

Section 8:
Evading Firewalls

Firewall Evasion Techniques Overview

Firewalls and intrusion prevention systems are designed to prevent tools like Nmap from getting an accurate picture of the systems they are protecting. Nmap includes a number of features designed to circumvent these defenses. This section discusses the various evasion techniques built into Nmap.

Summary of features covered in this section:

Feature	Option
Fragment Packets	-f
Specify a Specific MTU	--mtu
Use a Decoy	-D
Idle Zombie Scan	-sI
Manually Specify a Source Port	--source-port
Append Random Data	--data-length
Randomize Target Scan Order	--randomize-hosts
Spoof MAC Address	--spoof-mac
Send Bad Checksums	--badsum

Fragment Packets

The **-f** option is used to fragment probes into 8-byte packets.

Usage syntax: nmap -f [target]

```
# nmap -f 10.10.1.48

Starting Nmap 5.00 ( http://nmap.org ) at 2009-11-11 10:10 CST
Interesting ports on 10.10.1.48:
Not shown: 994 closed ports
PORT       STATE  SERVICE
21/tcp     open   ftp
22/tcp     open   ssh
25/tcp     open   smtp
80/tcp     open   http
111/tcp    open   rpcbind
2049/tcp   open   nfs
MAC Address: 00:0C:29:D5:38:F4 (VMware)

Nmap done: 1 IP address (1 host up) scanned in 1.52 seconds
```
Scanning a target using fragmented packets

The **-f** option instructs Nmap to send small 8-byte packets thus fragmenting the probe into many very small packets. This option isn't particularly useful in everyday situations; however, it may be helpful when attempting to evade some older or improperly configured firewalls.

> **Tip**
> Some host operating systems may require the use of **--send-eth** combined with **-f** for fragmented packets to be properly transmitted.

Specify a Specific MTU

The **--mtu** option is used to specify a custom MTU (Maximum Transmission Unit).

Usage syntax: nmap --mtu [number] [target]

```
# nmap --mtu 16 10.10.1.48

Starting Nmap 5.00 ( http://nmap.org ) at 2009-11-11 10:11 CST
Interesting ports on 10.10.1.48:
Not shown: 994 closed ports
PORT       STATE  SERVICE
21/tcp     open   ftp
22/tcp     open   ssh
25/tcp     open   smtp
80/tcp     open   http
111/tcp    open   rpcbind
2049/tcp   open   nfs
MAC Address: 00:0C:29:D5:38:F4 (VMware)

Nmap done: 1 IP address (1 host up) scanned in 0.34 seconds
```

Specifying a specific MTU

The **--mtu** option is similar to the **-f** option (discussed on page 117) except it allows you to specify your own MTU to be used during scanning. This creates fragmented packets that can potentially confuse some firewalls. In the above example, the **--mtu 16** argument instructs Nmap to use tiny 16-byte packets for the scan.

> **Note** *The MTU must be a multiple of 8 (example 8, 16, 24, 32, etc).*

> **Tip** *Some host operating systems may require the use of **--send-eth** combined with **--mtu** for fragmented packets to be properly transmitted.*

Use a Decoy

The **-D** option is used to mask an Nmap scan by using one or more decoys.

Usage syntax: nmap -D [decoy1,decoy2,etc|RND:number] [target]

```
# nmap -D RND:10 10.10.1.48

Starting Nmap 5.00 ( http://nmap.org ) at 2009-11-02 16:41 CST
...
```

Masking a scan using 10 randomly generated decoy IP addresses

When performing a decoy scan Nmap will spoof additional packets from the specified number of decoy addresses. This effectively makes it appear that the target is being scanned by multiple systems simultaneously. Using decoys allows the actual source of the scan to "blend into the crowd" which makes it harder to trace where the scan is coming from.

In the above example **nmap -D RND:10** instructs Nmap to generate 10 random decoys. You can also specify decoy addresses manually using the following syntax: **nmap -D decoy1,decoy2,decoy3,etc**.

Warning	*Using too many decoys can cause network congestion and reduce the effectiveness of a scan. Additionally, some internet service providers may filter spoofed traffic which will reduce the effectiveness of using decoys to cloak your scanning activity.*

119

Idle Zombie Scan

The **-sI** option is used to perform an idle zombie scan.

Usage syntax: nmap -sI [zombie host] [target]

```
# nmap -sI 10.10.1.41 10.10.1.252

Starting Nmap 5.00 ( http://nmap.org ) at 2009-11-14 18:35 CST
Idle scan using zombie 10.10.1.41 (10.10.1.41:443); Class: Incremental
Interesting ports on 10.10.1.252:
Not shown: 997 closed|filtered ports
PORT     STATE SERVICE
135/tcp  open  msrpc
139/tcp  open  netbios-ssn
445/tcp  open  microsoft-ds
MAC Address: 00:25:64:D7:FF:59 (Dell)

Nmap done: 1 IP address (1 host up) scanned in 8.29 seconds
```

Using an idle "zombie" to scan a target

The idle zombie scan is a unique scanning technique that allows you to exploit an idle system and use it to scan a target system for you. In this example 10.10.1.41 is the zombie and 10.10.1.252 is the target system. The scan works by exploiting the predictable IP sequence ID generation employed by some systems. In order for an idle scan to be successful, the zombie system must truly be idle at the time of scanning.

> **Note** With this scan no probe packets are sent from your system to the target; although an initial ping packet will be sent to the target unless you combine *-PN* with *-sI*.

More information about the idle zombie scan can be found on the Nmap website at www.nmap.org/book/idlescan.html.

Manually Specify a Source Port Number

The **--source-port** option is used to manually specify the source port number of a probe.

Usage syntax: nmap --source-port [port] [target]

```
# nmap --source-port 53 scanme.insecure.org

Starting Nmap 5.00 ( http://nmap.org ) at 2009-12-16 16:41 CST
Interesting ports on scanme.nmap.org (64.13.134.52):
Not shown: 993 filtered ports
PORT       STATE  SERVICE
25/tcp     closed smtp
53/tcp     open   domain
70/tcp     closed gopher
80/tcp     open   http
110/tcp    closed pop3
113/tcp    closed auth
31337/tcp  closed Elite

Nmap done: 1 IP address (1 host up) scanned in 7.59 seconds
```

Manually specifying the packet source port number

Every TCP segment contains a source port number in addition to a destination. By default, Nmap will randomly pick an available outgoing source port to probe a target. The **--source-port** option will force Nmap to use the specified port as the source for all packets. This technique can be used to exploit weaknesses in firewalls that are improperly configured to blindly accept incoming traffic based on a specific port number. Port 20 (FTP), port 53 (DNS), and 67 (DHCP) are common ports susceptible to this type of scan.

> **Tip** *The **-g** option is a shortcut that is synonymous with **--source-port**.*

Append Random Data

The **--data-length** option can be used to append random data to probe packets.

Usage syntax: nmap --data-length [number] [target]

```
# nmap --data-length 25 10.10.1.252

Starting Nmap 5.00 ( http://nmap.org ) at 2009-11-14 18:41 CST
Interesting ports on 10.10.1.252:
Not shown: 995 filtered ports
PORT      STATE SERVICE
135/tcp   open  msrpc
139/tcp   open  netbios-ssn
445/tcp   open  microsoft-ds
5800/tcp  open  vnc-http
5900/tcp  open  vnc
MAC Address: 00:25:64:D7:FF:59 (Dell)

Nmap done: 1 IP address (1 host up) scanned in 5.17 seconds
```

Padding a scan with random data to avoid detection

Nmap transmits packets which are generally a specific size. Some firewall vendors know to look for this type of predictable packet size. The **--data-length** option adds the specified amount of additional data to probes in an effort to circumvent these types of checks. In the above example 25 additional bytes are added to all packets sent to the target.

Randomize Target Scan Order

The **--randomize-hosts** option is used to randomize the scanning order of the specified targets.

Usage syntax: nmap --randomize-hosts [targets]

```
$ nmap --randomize-hosts 10.10.1.100-254

Interesting ports on 10.10.1.109:
Not shown: 996 filtered ports
PORT      STATE SERVICE
139/tcp   open  netbios-ssn
445/tcp   open  microsoft-ds
5800/tcp  open  vnc-http
5900/tcp  open  vnc
MAC Address: 00:1C:23:49:75:0C (Dell)

Interesting ports on 10.10.1.100:
Not shown: 996 filtered ports
PORT      STATE SERVICE
139/tcp   open  netbios-ssn
445/tcp   open  microsoft-ds
5800/tcp  open  vnc-http
5900/tcp  open  vnc
MAC Address: 00:21:9B:3F:AC:EC (Dell)

Interesting ports on 10.10.1.107:
Not shown: 997 closed ports
PORT      STATE SERVICE
22/tcp   open  ssh
139/tcp  open  netbios-ssn
...
```

Scanning systems in a random order

The **--randomize-hosts** option helps prevent scans of multiple targets from being detected by firewalls and intrusion detection systems. This is done by scanning them in a random order instead of sequential.

Spoof MAC Address

The **--spoof-mac** is used to spoof the MAC (Media Access Control) address of an ethernet device.

Usage syntax: `nmap --spoof-mac [vendor|MAC|0] [target]`

```
# nmap -sT -PN --spoof-mac 0 192.168.1.1

Starting Nmap 5.00 ( http://nmap.org ) at 2010-01-15 19:48 CST
Spoofing MAC address 00:01:02:25:56:AE (3com)
Interesting ports on 192.168.1.1:
Not shown: 995 filtered ports
PORT      STATE  SERVICE
20/tcp    closed ftp-data
21/tcp    closed ftp
23/tcp    closed telnet
80/tcp    open   http
2869/tcp  open   unknown

Nmap done: 1 IP address (1 host up) scanned in 4.78 seconds
```

Using a spoofed MAC address

In this example, Nmap is instructed to forge a randomly generated 3com MAC address. This makes your scanning activity harder to trace by preventing your MAC address from being logged on the target system.

The **--spoof-mac** option can be controlled by the following parameters:

Argument	Function
0 (zero)	Generates a random MAC address
Specific MAC Address	Uses the specified MAC address
Vendor Name	Generates a MAC address from the specified vendor (such as Apple, Dell, 3Com, etc)

MAC address spoofing options

Send Bad Checksums

The **--badsum** option is used to send packets with incorrect checksums to the specified host.

Usage syntax: nmap --badsum [target]

```
# nmap --badsum 10.10.1.41

Starting Nmap 5.00 ( http://nmap.org ) at 2009-08-24 16:19 CDT
All 1000 scanned ports on 10.10.1.41 are filtered
MAC Address: 00:60:B0:59:B6:14 (Hewlett-packard CO.)

Nmap done: 1 IP address (1 host up) scanned in 21.40 seconds
```

Scanning a target using bad checksums

The TCP/IP protocol uses checksums to ensure data integrity. Crafting packets with bad checksums can, in some rare occasions, produce a response from a poorly configured system. In the above example we did not receive any results, meaning the target system is configured correctly. This is a typical result when using the **--badsum** option.

Note	Only a poorly configured system would respond to a packet with a bad checksum. Nevertheless, it is a good tool to use when auditing network security or attempting to evade firewalls.

125

Section 9:
Output Options

Output Options Overview

Nmap offers several options for creating formatted output. In addition to displaying the standard output on a screen, you can also save scan results in a text file, XML file, or a single line grepable file. This feature can be helpful when scanning a large number of systems or for comparing the results of two scans using the **ndiff** utility (discussed in Section 13).

> **Note**
>
> The **grep** pattern matching utility is only available on Unix, Linux, and Mac OS X systems by default. Windows users can download a Win32 port of the GNU grep program at http://gnuwin32.sourceforge.net to use with the examples discussed in this section.

Summary of features covered in this section:

Feature	Option
Save Output to a Text File	-oN
Save Output to a XML File	-oX
Grepable Output	-oG
Output All Supported File Types	-oA
Periodically Display Statistics	--stats-every
133t Output	-oS

Save Output to a Text File

The **-oN** parameter saves the results of a scan in a plain text file.

Usage syntax: nmap -oN [scan.txt] [target]

```
$ nmap -oN scan.txt 10.10.1.1

Starting Nmap 5.00 ( http://nmap.org ) at 2009-08-13 15:17 CDT
Interesting ports on 10.10.1.1:
Not shown: 998 closed ports
PORT     STATE SERVICE
80/tcp   open  http
443/tcp  open  https

Nmap done: 1 IP address (1 host up) scanned in 0.47 seconds
```

Saving Nmap output in a text file

The results of the above scan are saved to the scan.txt file shown below.

```
$ cat scan.txt
# Nmap 5.00 scan initiated Thu Aug 13 15:17:16 2009 as: nmap -oN
scan.txt 10.10.1.1
Interesting ports on 10.10.1.1:
Not shown: 998 closed ports
PORT     STATE SERVICE
80/tcp   open  http
443/tcp  open  https

# Nmap done at Thu Aug 13 15:17:17 2009 -- 1 IP address (1 host up)
scanned in 0.47 seconds
```

Reviewing the contents of the scan.txt file

> **Note:** Nmap will overwrite an existing output file unless the *--append-output* option is combined with *-oN*.

129

Save Output to a XML File

The **-oX** parameter saves the results of a scan in a XML file.

Usage syntax: nmap -oX [scan.xml] [target]

```
$ nmap -oX scan.xml 10.10.1.1

Starting Nmap 5.00 ( http://nmap.org ) at 2009-08-13 15:19 CDT
Interesting ports on 10.10.1.1:
Not shown: 998 closed ports
PORT     STATE SERVICE
80/tcp   open  http
443/tcp  open  https
...
```
Creating a XML output file

The results of the above scan are saved to the scan.xml file shown below.

```
$ cat scan.xml
<?xml version="1.0" ?>
<?xml-stylesheet href="file:///usr/local/share/nmap/nmap.xsl"
type="text/xsl"?>
<!-- Nmap 5.00 scan initiated Thu Aug 13 15:19:44 2009 as: nmap -oX
scan.xml 10.10.1.1 -->
<nmaprun scanner="nmap" args="nmap -oX scan.xml 10.10.1.1"
start="1250194784" startstr="Thu Aug 13 15:19:44 2009" version="5.00"
...
```
Viewing the contents of the XML output file

The resulting XML file has hardcoded file paths which may only work the system where the file was created. The **--webxml** parameter can be combined with **-oX** to create a portable file for any system (with internet access). You can also specify an alternative style sheet using the **--stylesheet** parameter. To avoid referencing a style sheet at all, use the **--no-stylesheet** parameter.

Grepable Output

The **-oG** option enables grepable output.

Usage syntax: nmap -oG [scan.txt] [target]

```
$ nmap -oG scan.txt -F -O 10.10.1.1/24

Starting Nmap 5.00 ( http://nmap.org ) at 2009-08-13 15:50 CDT
Interesting ports on 10.10.1.1:
Not shown: 998 closed ports
PORT     STATE SERVICE
80/tcp   open  http
443/tcp  open  https
...
```

Creating a grepable output file

The resulting scan is saved to the specified text file, which can be useful when combined with text parsing tools like Perl or **grep** (as displayed below).

```
$ grep "Windows 98" scan.txt
Host: 10.10.1.217 Ports: 139/open/tcp//netbios-ssn///,
5800/open/tcp//vnc-http///, 5900/open/tcp//vnc///   Ignored State:
closed (97)    OS: Microsoft Windows 98 SE    Seq Index: 18    IP ID
Seq: Broken little-endian incremental
...
```

Using the grep utility to review a Nmap output file

In the above example, the **grep** utility will display all instances of the specified text found in the scan.txt file. This makes it simple to quickly search for specific information when analyzing results from a large scan.

Output All Supported File Types

The **-oA** parameter saves the output of a scan in text, grepable, and XML formats.

Usage syntax: nmap -oA [filename] [target]

```
$ nmap -oA scans 10.10.1.1

Starting Nmap 5.00 ( http://nmap.org ) at 2009-08-13 16:10 CDT
Interesting ports on 10.10.1.1:
Not shown: 998 closed ports
PORT     STATE SERVICE
80/tcp   open  http
443/tcp  open  https

Nmap done: 1 IP address (1 host up) scanned in 0.66 seconds
```

Creating output files for all available formats

The resulting scan's output files are created with their respective extensions as displayed below.

```
$ ls -l scans.*
-rw-r--r-- 1 nick nick  284 2009-08-13 16:22 scans.gnmap
-rw-r--r-- 1 nick nick  307 2009-08-13 16:22 scans.nmap
-rw-r--r-- 1 nick nick 5150 2009-08-13 16:22 scans.xml
```

Directory listing of the resulting output files

File	Contents
scans.gnmap	Grepable output
scans.nmap	Plain text output
scans.xml	XML output

Nmap output files

Display Scan Statistics

The **--stats-every** option can be used to periodically display the status of the current scan.

Usage syntax: nmap --stats-every [time] [target]

```
$ nmap --stats-every 5s 10.10.1.41

Starting Nmap 5.00 ( http://nmap.org ) at 2009-08-13 16:30 CDT
Stats: 0:00:07 elapsed; 0 hosts completed (1 up), 1 undergoing Service Scan
Service scan Timing: About 55.00% done; ETC: 16:30 (0:00:05 remaining)
Stats: 0:00:12 elapsed; 0 hosts completed (1 up), 1 undergoing Service Scan
Service scan Timing: About 85.00% done; ETC: 16:30 (0:00:02 remaining)
Stats: 0:00:17 elapsed; 0 hosts completed (1 up), 1 undergoing Service Scan
Service scan Timing: About 90.00% done; ETC: 16:30 (0:00:02 remaining)
Stats: 0:00:22 elapsed; 0 hosts completed (1 up), 1 undergoing Service Scan
Service scan Timing: About 90.00% done; ETC: 16:30 (0:00:02 remaining)
Stats: 0:00:27 elapsed; 0 hosts completed (1 up), 1 undergoing Service Scan
Service scan Timing: About 90.00% done; ETC: 16:30 (0:00:03 remaining)
Stats: 0:00:32 elapsed; 0 hosts completed (1 up), 1 undergoing Service Scan
...
```

Nmap scan status output

On slow scans you may get bored looking at your screen doing nothing for long periods of time. The **--stats-every** option can alleviate this problem. In the above example, **--stats-every 5s** instructs Nmap to display the status of the current scan every five seconds. Timing parameters can be specified in seconds (s), minutes (m), or hours (h) by appending an s, m, or h to the interval number as described on page 99.

133t Output

The **-oS** option enables "script kiddie" output.

Usage syntax: nmap -oS [scan.txt] [target]

```
$ nmap -oS scan.txt 10.10.1.1

Starting Nmap 5.00 ( http://nmap.org ) at 2009-08-13 15:45 CDT
Interesting ports on 10.10.1.1:
Not shown: 998 closed ports
PORT     STATE SERVICE
80/tcp   open  http
443/tcp  open  https

Nmap done: 1 IP address (1 host up) scanned in 0.48 seconds
```
Creating a "133t" output file

Script kiddie or "leet" speak is output is a cryptic form of typing used mostly by immature teenagers on message boards and chat sites. This option is included as a joke and isn't really useful for anything other than a good laugh. The results of the **-oS** option are saved in scan.txt file displayed below.

```
$ cat scan.txt

StaRtING NMap 5.00 ( hTtp://nmap.oRg ) aT 2009-08-13 15:45 CDT
!nt3r3St|ng pOrts On 10.10.1.1:
n0t $h0wn: 998 cl0$3d p0rt$
PORT     $TATE seRV!CE
80/tcp   Open  hTtp
443/tcp  Open  httpS

Nmap DOnE: 1 Ip addresz (1 host up) $canned iN 0.48 $3c0nds
```
Nmap script kiddie output

Section 10:

Troubleshooting and Debugging

Troubleshooting and Debugging Overview

Technical problems are an inherent part of using computers. Nmap is no exception. Occasionally a scan may not produce the output you expected; you may receive an error – or you may not receive any output at all. Nmap offers several options for tracing and debugging a scan which can help identify why this happens. The following section describes these troubleshooting and debugging features in detail.

Summary of features covered in this section:

Feature	Option
Getting Help	-h
Display Nmap Version	-V
Verbose Output	-v
Debugging	-d
Display Port State Reason	--reason
Only Display Open Ports	--open
Trace Packets	--packet-trace
Display Host Networking	--iflist
Specify a Network Interface	-e

Getting Help

Executing **nmap -h** will display a summary of available options.

Usage syntax: nmap -h

```
$ nmap -h
Nmap 5.00 ( http://nmap.org )
Usage: nmap [Scan Type(s)] {target specification}
TARGET SPECIFICATION:
  Can pass hostnames, IP addresses, networks, etc.
  Ex: scanme.nmap.org, microsoft.com/24, 192.168.0.1; 10.0.0-255.1-254
  -iL <inputfilename>: Input from list of hosts/networks
  -iR <num hosts>: Choose random targets
  --exclude <host1[,host2][,host3],...>: Exclude hosts/networks
  --excludefile <exclude_file>: Exclude list from file
...
```

Displaying Nmap help information

For more detailed information you can read the Nmap manual page by typing **man nmap** on the command line.

```
$ man nmap
```

Accessing the Nmap man page on Unix and Linux systems

Note	The **man** command is only available on Unix, Linux, and Mac OS X based systems. Windows users can read the Nmap manual online at www.nmap.org/book/man.html.

Tip	You can also find help online by subscribing to the Nmap mailing list at www.seclists.org.

Display Nmap Version

The **-V** option is used to display the installed version of Nmap.

Usage syntax: nmap -V

```
$ nmap -V
Nmap version 5.00 ( http://nmap.org )
```

Displaying the installed version of Nmap

When troubleshooting Nmap problems you should always make sure you have the most up-to-date version installed. Open source programs like Nmap are developed at a rapid pace and bugs are typically fixed as soon as they are discovered. Compare your installed version to the latest version available on the Nmap website at www.nmap.org to make sure you are running the most up-to-date version available. This will ensure that you have access to the latest features as well as the most bug-free version available.

Verbose Output

The **-v** option is used to enable verbose output.

Usage syntax: nmap -v [target]

```
$ nmap -v scanme.insecure.org

Starting Nmap 5.00 ( http://nmap.org ) at 2009-08-12 15:06 CDT
NSE: Loaded 0 scripts for scanning.
Initiating Ping Scan at 15:06
Scanning 64.13.134.52 [2 ports]
Completed Ping Scan at 15:06, 1.87s elapsed (1 total hosts)
Initiating Parallel DNS resolution of 1 host. at 15:06
Completed Parallel DNS resolution of 1 host. at 15:06, 0.16s elapsed
Initiating Connect Scan at 15:06
Scanning scanme.nmap.org (64.13.134.52) [1000 ports]
Discovered open port 53/tcp on 64.13.134.52
Discovered open port 80/tcp on 64.13.134.52
Completed Connect Scan at 15:06, 7.00s elapsed (1000 total ports)
Host scanme.nmap.org (64.13.134.52) is up (0.087s latency).
Interesting ports on scanme.nmap.org (64.13.134.52):
Not shown: 998 filtered ports
PORT     STATE  SERVICE
53/tcp   open   domain
80/tcp   open   http

Read data files from: /usr/local/share/nmap
Nmap done: 1 IP address (1 host up) scanned in 9.41 seconds
```

Nmap scan with verbose output enabled

Verbose output can be useful when troubleshooting connectivity problems, or if you are simply interested in what's going on behind the scenes of your scan.

> **Tip** *You can use the **-v** option twice (**-v -v** or **-vv**) to enable additional verbose output.*

Debugging

The **-d** option enables debugging output.

Usage syntax: nmap -d[1-9] [target]

```
$ nmap -d scanme.insecure.org

Starting Nmap 5.00 ( http://nmap.org ) at 2009-08-12 15:26 CDT
PORTS: Using top 1000 ports found open (TCP:1000, UDP:0, SCTP:0)
--------------- Timing report ---------------
  hostgroups: min 1, max 100000
  rtt-timeouts: init 1000, min 100, max 10000
  max-scan-delay: TCP 1000, UDP 1000, SCTP 1000
  parallelism: min 0, max 0
  max-retries: 10, host-timeout: 0
  min-rate: 0, max-rate: 0
---------------------------------------------
NSE: Loaded 0 scripts for scanning.
Initiating Ping Scan at 15:26
Scanning 64.13.134.52 [2 ports]
Completed Ping Scan at 15:26, 2.83s elapsed (1 total hosts)
Overall sending rates: 1.06 packets / s.
mass_rdns: Using DNS server 10.10.1.44
mass_rdns: Using DNS server 10.10.1.45
Initiating Parallel DNS resolution of 1 host. at 15:26
mass_rdns: 0.00s 0/1 [#: 2, OK: 0, NX: 0, DR: 0, SF: 0, TR: 1]
Completed Parallel DNS resolution of 1 host. at 15:26, 0.00s elapsed
...
```

Nmap debugging output

Debugging output provides additional information that can be use to trace bugs or troubleshoot problems. The default **-d** output provides a fair amount of debugging information. You can also specify a debugging level of 1-9 to be used with the **-d** parameter to increase or decrease the amount of output. For example: **-d1** provides the lowest amount of debugging output and **-d9** is the highest.

Display Port State Reason Codes

The **--reason** parameter displays the reason why a port is considered to be in the given state.

Usage syntax: nmap --reason [target]

```
$ nmap --reason scanme.insecure.org

Starting Nmap 5.00 ( http://nmap.org ) at 2009-08-12 15:43 CDT
Interesting ports on scanme.nmap.org (64.13.134.52):
Not shown: 993 filtered ports
Reason: 993 no-responses
PORT        STATE  SERVICE REASON
25/tcp      closed smtp    conn-refused
53/tcp      open   domain  syn-ack
70/tcp      closed gopher  conn-refused
80/tcp      open   http    syn-ack
110/tcp     closed pop3    conn-refused
113/tcp     closed auth    conn-refused
31337/tcp   closed Elite   conn-refused

Nmap done: 1 IP address (1 host up) scanned in 8.83 seconds
```
Nmap scan with port state reason codes enabled

Notice the addition of the reason field in the above scan. Information in this field can be useful when trying to determine why a target's ports are in a particular state. Ports that respond with *syn-ack* are considered to be open. Ports that respond with *conn-refuse*d or *reset* are typically closed. Ports that do not respond at all are generally filtered (by a firewall).

Only Display Open Ports

The **--open** parameter instructs Nmap to only display open ports.

Usage syntax: nmap --open [target]

```
$ nmap --open scanme.insecure.org

Starting Nmap 5.00 ( http://nmap.org ) at 2009-12-18 12:47 CST
Interesting ports on scanme.nmap.org (64.13.134.52):
Not shown: 993 filtered ports, 5 closed ports
PORT     STATE SERVICE
53/tcp   open  domain
80/tcp   open  http

Nmap done: 1 IP address (1 host up) scanned in 8.26 second
```
Limiting Nmap output to display open ports only

The **--open** parameter removes closed and filtered ports from the scan results. This option is useful when you want to unclutter the results of your scan so that only open ports are displayed. The same scan without the **--open** option is displayed below for comparison.

```
$ nmap scanme.insecure.org

Starting Nmap 5.00 ( http://nmap.org ) at 2009-12-18 12:49 CST
Interesting ports on scanme.nmap.org (64.13.134.52):
Not shown: 993 filtered ports
PORT      STATE   SERVICE
25/tcp    closed  smtp
53/tcp    open    domain
70/tcp    closed  gopher
80/tcp    open    http
110/tcp   closed  pop3
113/tcp   closed  auth
...
```
Nmap scan displaying open and closed ports

Trace Packets

The **--packet-trace** parameter instructs Nmap to display a summary of all packets sent and received.

Usage syntax: nmap --packet-trace [target]

```
$ nmap --packet-trace 10.10.1.1
Starting Nmap 5.00 ( http://nmap.org ) at 2009-08-13 17:14 CDT
CONN (0.1600s) TCP localhost > 10.10.1.1:80 => Operation now in progress
CONN (0.1600s) TCP localhost > 10.10.1.1:443 => Operation now in progress
NSOCK (0.1610s) UDP connection requested to 10.10.1.45:53 (IOD #1) EID 8
NSOCK (0.1610s) Read request from IOD #1 [10.10.1.45:53] (timeout: -1ms) EID 18
NSOCK (0.1610s) UDP connection requested to 10.10.1.44:53 (IOD #2) EID 24
NSOCK (0.1610s) Read request from IOD #2 [10.10.1.44:53] (timeout: -1ms) EID 34
NSOCK (0.1610s) Write request for 40 bytes to IOD #1 EID 43 [10.10.1.45:53]:
V!..........1.1.10.10.in-addr.arpa.....
NSOCK (0.1610s) nsock_loop() started (timeout=500ms). 5 events pending
NSOCK (0.1610s) Callback: CONNECT SUCCESS for EID 8 [10.10.1.45:53]
NSOCK (0.1610s) Callback: CONNECT SUCCESS for EID 24 [10.10.1.44:53]
NSOCK (0.1610s) Callback: WRITE SUCCESS for EID 43 [10.10.1.45:53]
...
```

Packet trace output

The **--packet-trace** parameter is another useful tool for troubleshooting connectivity issues. The example above displays detailed information about every packet sent to and received from the target system.

> **Tip:** *Trace information will rapidly scroll across the screen. See page 129 for information about saving trace data to a file for easier viewing.*

Display Host Networking Configuration

The **--iflist** option displays the network interfaces and routes configured on the local system.

Usage syntax: `nmap --iflist`

```
$ nmap --iflist

Starting Nmap 5.00 ( http://nmap.org ) at 2009-08-13 17:03 CDT
************************INTERFACES************************
DEV    (SHORT) IP/MASK         TYPE      UP MAC
lo     (lo)    127.0.0.1/8     loopback  up
eth0   (eth0)  10.10.1.107/24  ethernet  up 00:21:70:AC:F7:E7
wlan0  (wlan0) 10.10.1.176/24  ethernet  up 00:16:EA:F0:92:50


**************************ROUTES**************************
DST/MASK        DEV    GATEWAY
10.10.1.0/0     eth0
10.10.1.0/0     wlan0
169.254.0.0/0   wlan0
0.0.0.0/0       eth0   10.10.1.1
```

Interface list output

The above example displays the general network and routing information for the local system. This option can be helpful for quickly identifying network information or troubleshooting connectivity issues.

> **Tip**
> *Additional commands that are helpful for troubleshooting networking configuration include **ifconfig** (Unix/Linux) and **ipconfig** (Windows). Most Windows and Unix based systems also include the **netstat** command which can provide additional network information.*

Specify Which Network Interface to Use

The **-e** option is used to manually specify which network interface Nmap should use.

Usage syntax: nmap -e [interface] [target]

```
$ nmap -e eth0 10.10.1.48

Starting Nmap 5.00 ( http://nmap.org ) at 2009-08-25 08:30 CDT
Interesting ports on 10.10.1.48:
Not shown: 994 closed ports
PORT       STATE  SERVICE
21/tcp     open   ftp
22/tcp     open   ssh
25/tcp     open   smtp
80/tcp     open   http
111/tcp    open   rpcbind
2049/tcp   open   nfs

Nmap done: 1 IP address (1 host up) scanned in 0.41 seconds
```
Manually specifying a network interface

Many systems have multiple network interfaces. Most modern laptops, for example, have both a regular ethernet jack and a wireless card. If you want to ensure Nmap is using your preferred interface you can use **-e** to specify it on the command line. In this example **-e** is used to force Nmap to scan via the *eth0* interface on the multi-homed host system.

Section 11:

Zenmap

Zenmap Overview

Zenmap is a graphical frontend for Nmap designed to make light work of Nmap's complex scanning features. The Zenmap GUI is a cross-platform program that can be used on Windows, Mac OS X, and Unix/Linux systems.

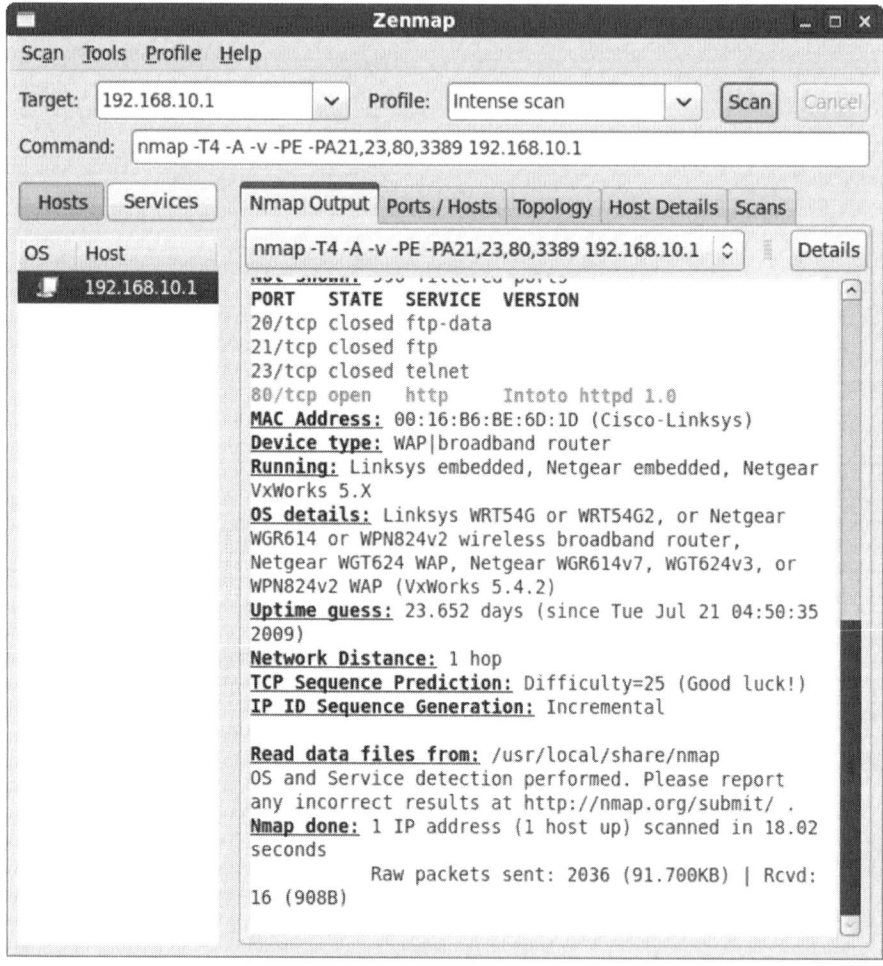

Zenmap GUI

Launching Zenmap

Windows Users

Zenmap is installed by default when you install Nmap on Windows systems. To start Zenmap go to **Start > Programs > Nmap > Zenmap GUI**.

Unix and Linux Users

Zenmap is automatically installed when you compile Nmap from source. If you install Nmap via **apt** or **yum** you may have to manually install the Zenmap package. This can be done by executing one of the following commands:

Debian/Ubuntu:	apt-get install zenmap
Fedora/Red Hat/CentOS:	yum install zenmap
Gentoo:	emerge zenmap

Once installed, the Zenmap GUI which can be launched by selecting **Applications > Internet > Zenmap** from the Gnome menu.

Mac OS X Users

Zenmap for Mac OS X is installed in **Applications > Zenmap**. It is included automatically as part of the default Nmap installation.

> **Note** *The X11 server for Mac OS X is required to run Zenmap on Mac systems. This software can be found on the Mac OS X installation DVD.*

Basic Zenmap Operations

Performing a scan with Zenmap is as simple as 1, 2, 3...

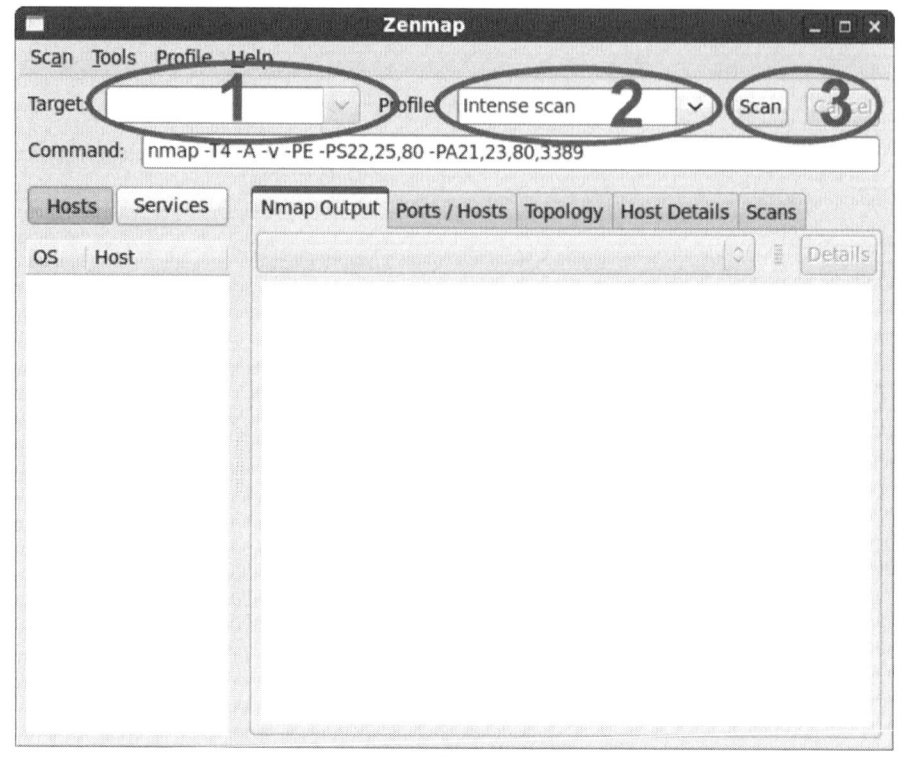

Zenmap GUI overview

Step 1: Enter a target (or select a recent target from the list)
Step 2: Select a scanning profile
Step 3: Press the scan button

Zenmap Results

The results of the scan are displayed once the scan is finished. The **Nmap Output** tab displays the raw output of the scan as it would appear on the command line.

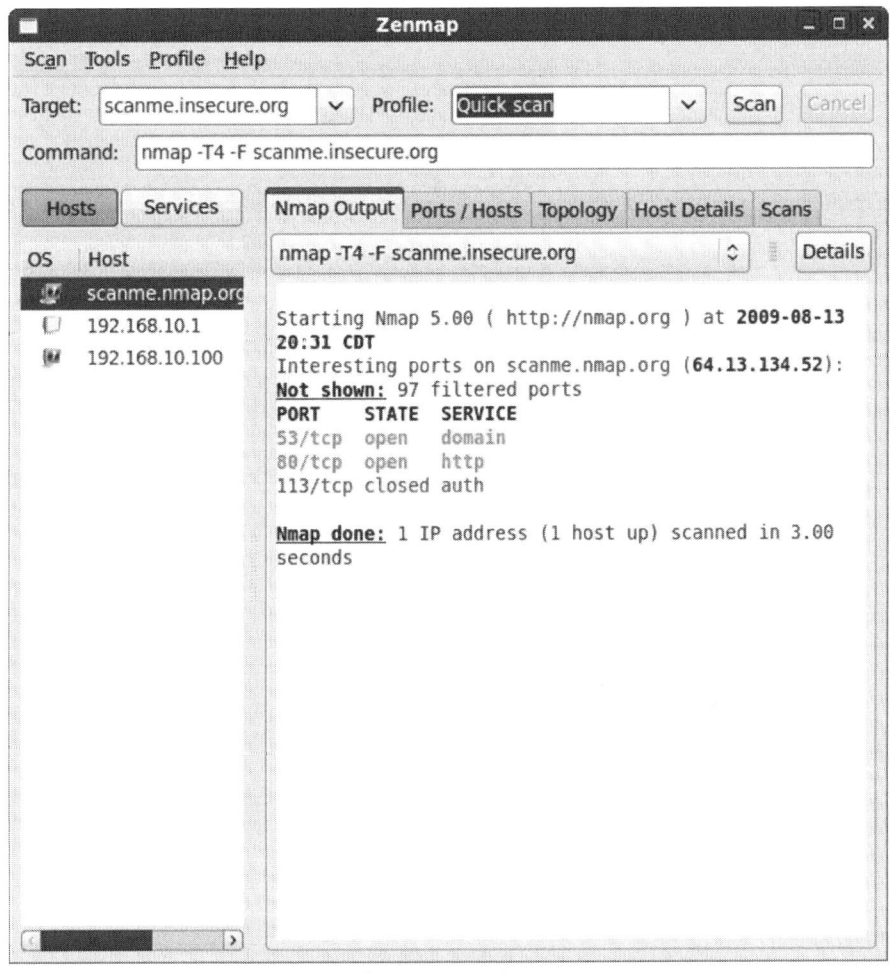

Zenmap scan output

> **Note:** *The actual command line string executed is displayed in the **Command** box above.*

Scanning Profiles

Zenmap provides built-in profiles for the most common types of scans. This simplifies the scanning process by eliminating the need to manually specify a long string of arguments on the command line.

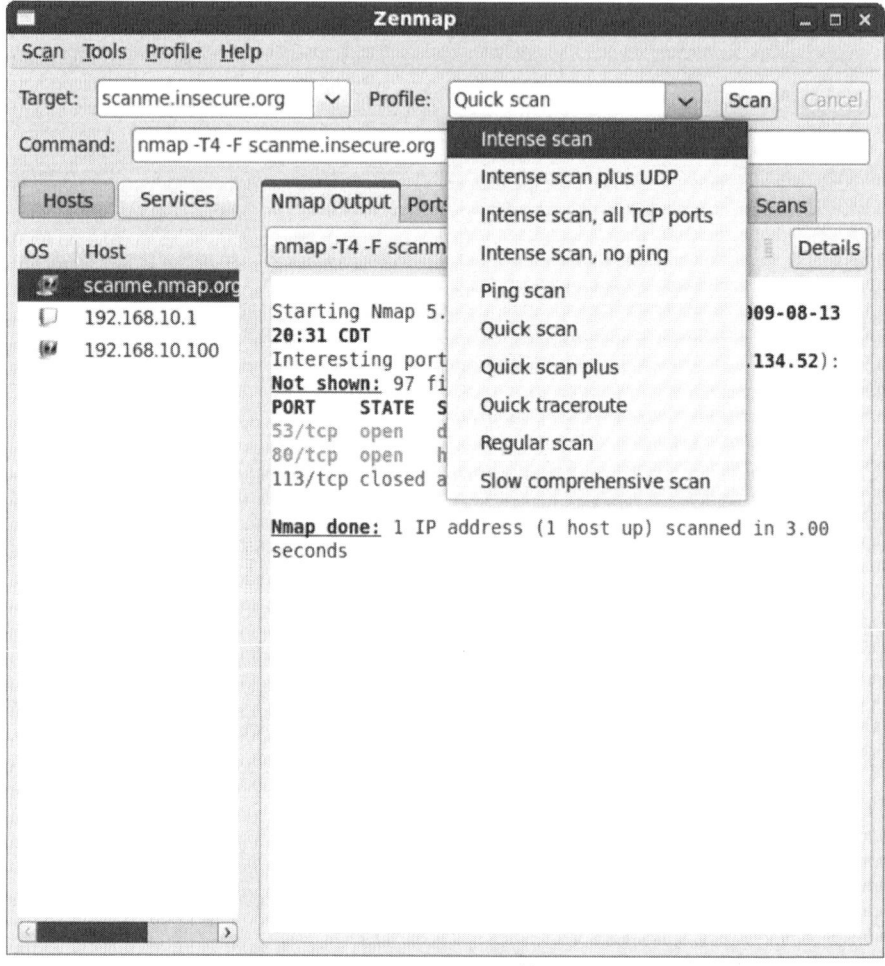

Zenmap scanning profiles

Profile Editor

If the built-in scans don't meet your exact needs, you can create your own scan profile. To do this, simply access the profile editor by selecting **Profile > New Profile** from the Zenmap menu (or press **CTRL + P** on the keyboard).

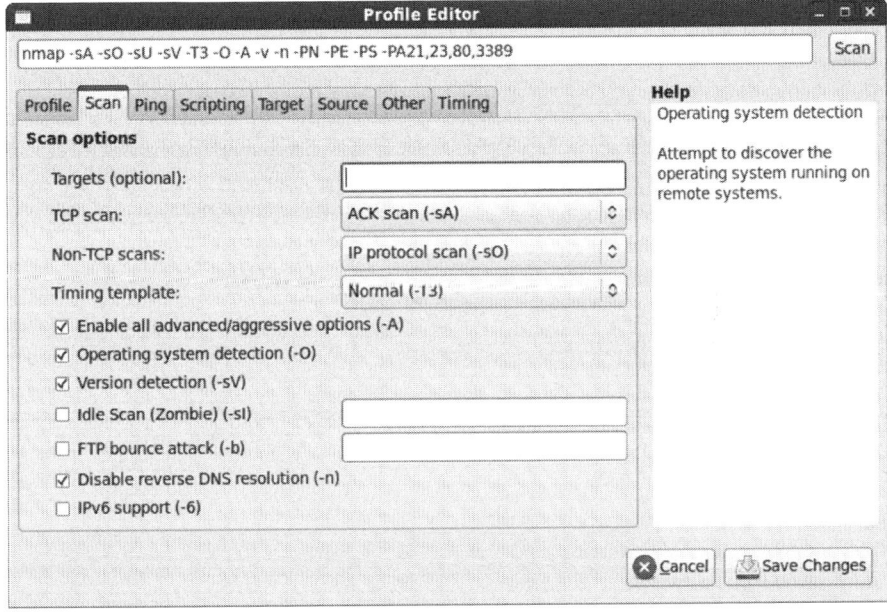

Zenmap profile editor

Within the Zenmap Profile Editor, you can select the options for your custom profile and Zenmap will automatically build the complex Nmap command line strings based on your selections.

Once finished, simply click the **Save Changes** button and your custom profile will be available for use in the profile selection menu.

Viewing Open Ports

Once a scan is completed you can view a user-friendly display of the results on the **Ports/Hosts** tab. The buttons labeled **Hosts** and **Services** can be used to toggle the display of the recent scans.

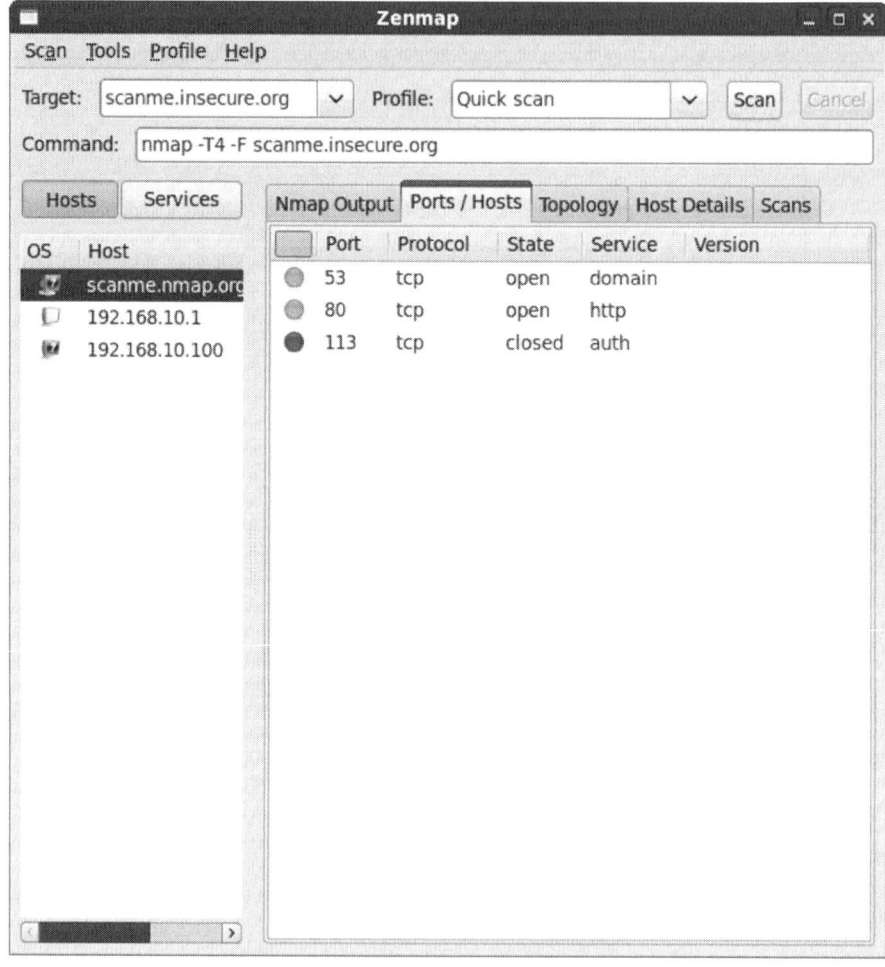

```
Zenmap
Scan  Tools  Profile  Help
Target: scanme.insecure.org    Profile: Quick scan       Scan  Cancel
Command: nmap -T4 -F scanme.insecure.org

Hosts | Services    Nmap Output | Ports / Hosts | Topology | Host Details | Scans

OS  Host                Port   Protocol   State    Service   Version
    scanme.nmap.org     53     tcp        open     domain
    192.168.10.1        80     tcp        open     http
    192.168.10.100      113    tcp        closed   auth
```

Zenmap ports display

Viewing a Network Map

After performing one or more scans, you can view the results on a graphical map on the **Topology** tab.

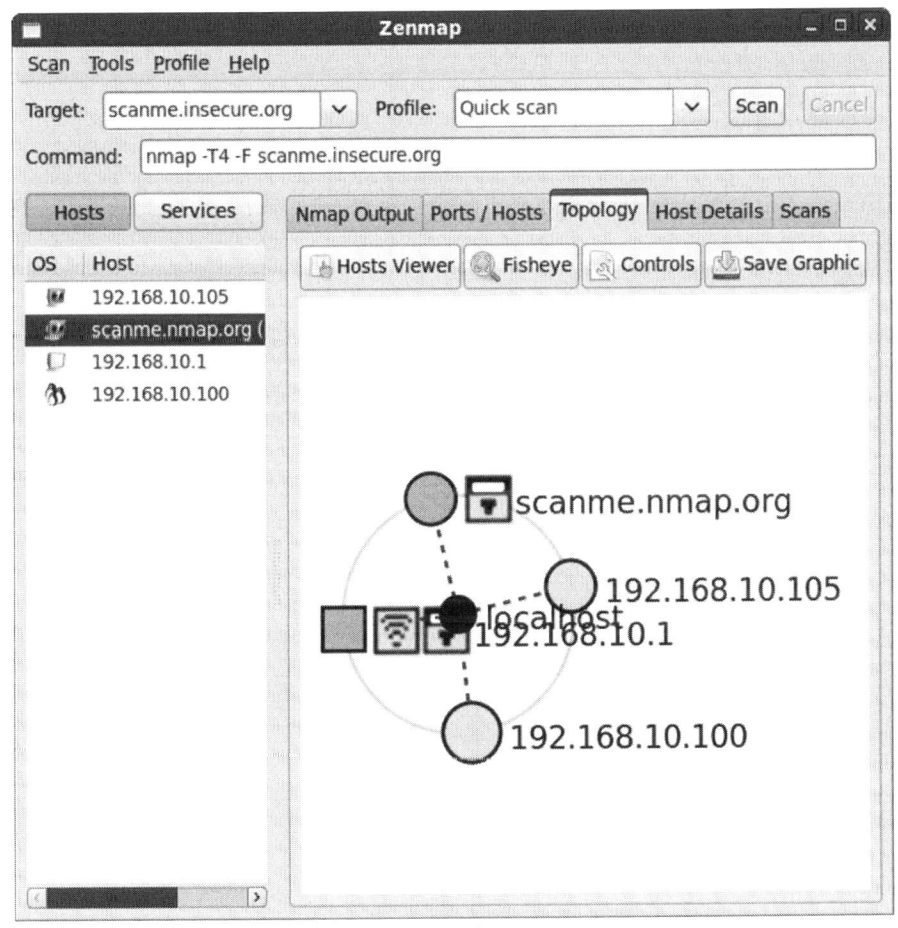

Zenmap topology map

Zenmap's topology feature provides an interactive graphic which can be manipulated by pressing the **Controls** button to modify the various display options.

155

Saving Network Maps

You can also save a Zenmap topology map by pressing the **Save Graphic** button.

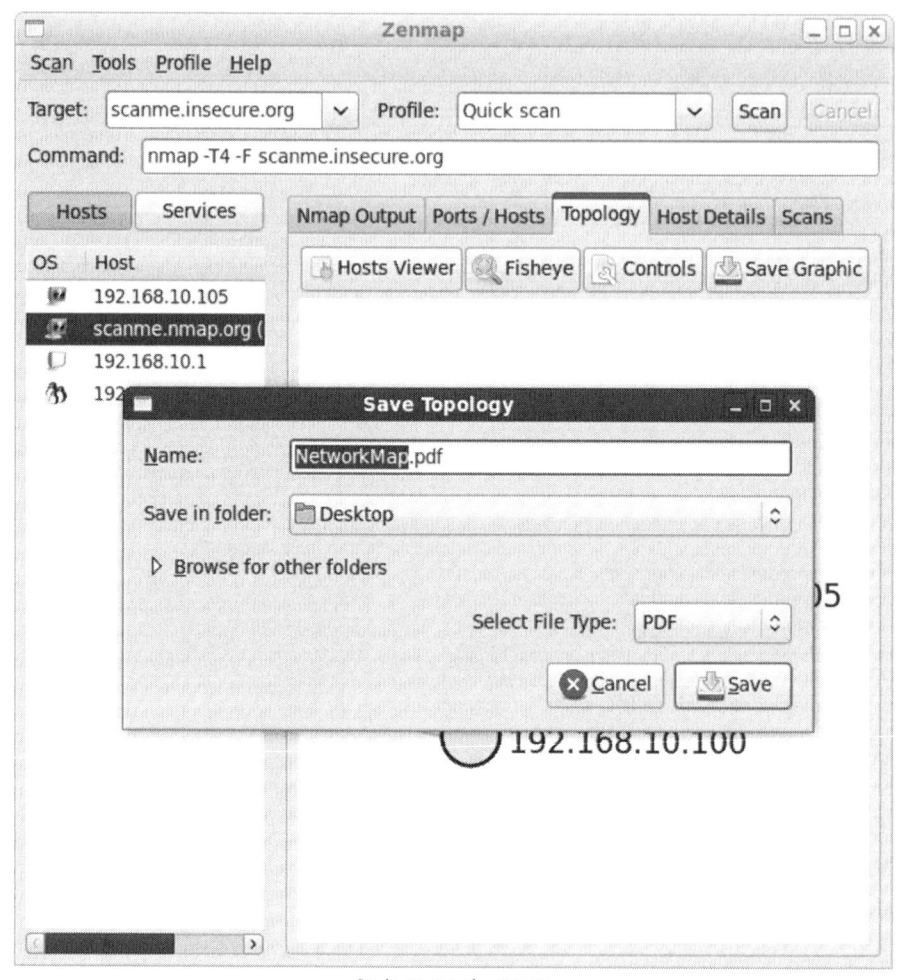

Saving a topology map

Zenmap supports exporting maps to several popular formats including PNG, PDF, SVG, and Postscript.

Viewing Host Details

The **Host Details** tab provides a user-friendly display of information gathered from a target system.

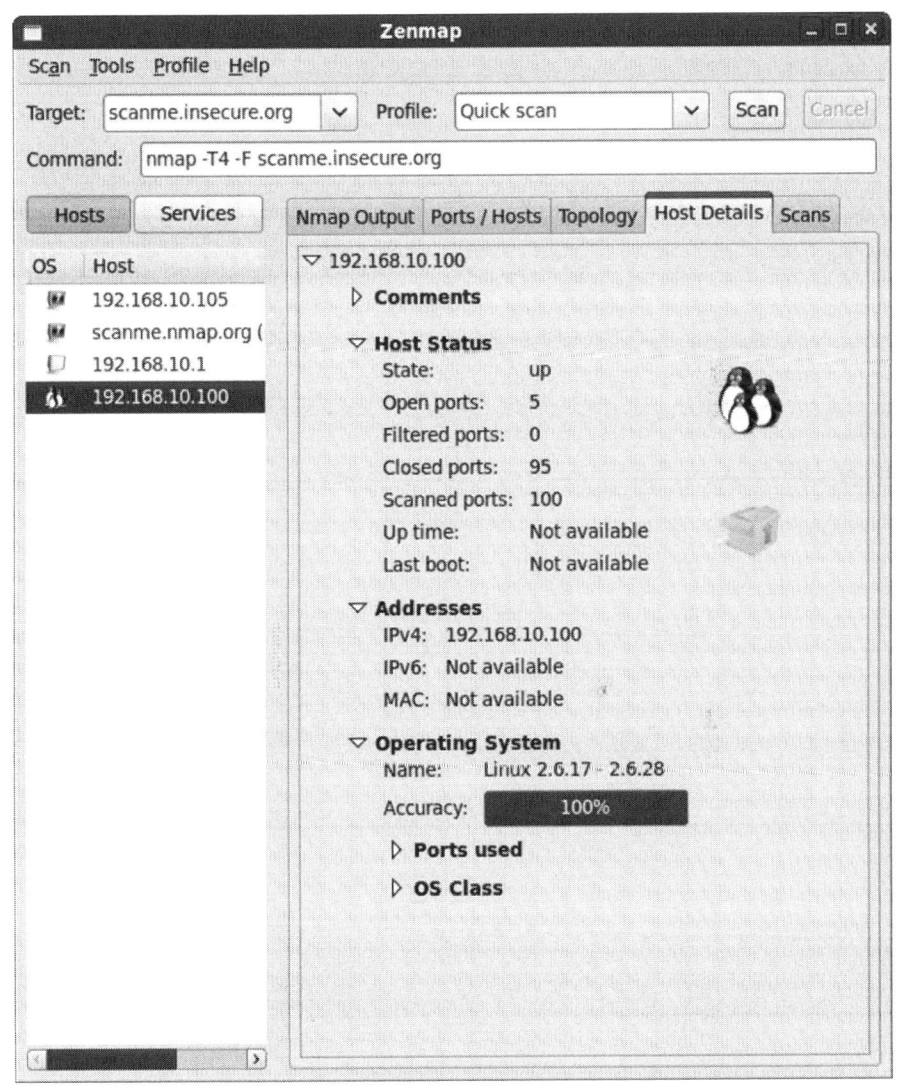

Zenmap host details

Viewing Scan History

The **Scans** tab displays scanning history for the current session.

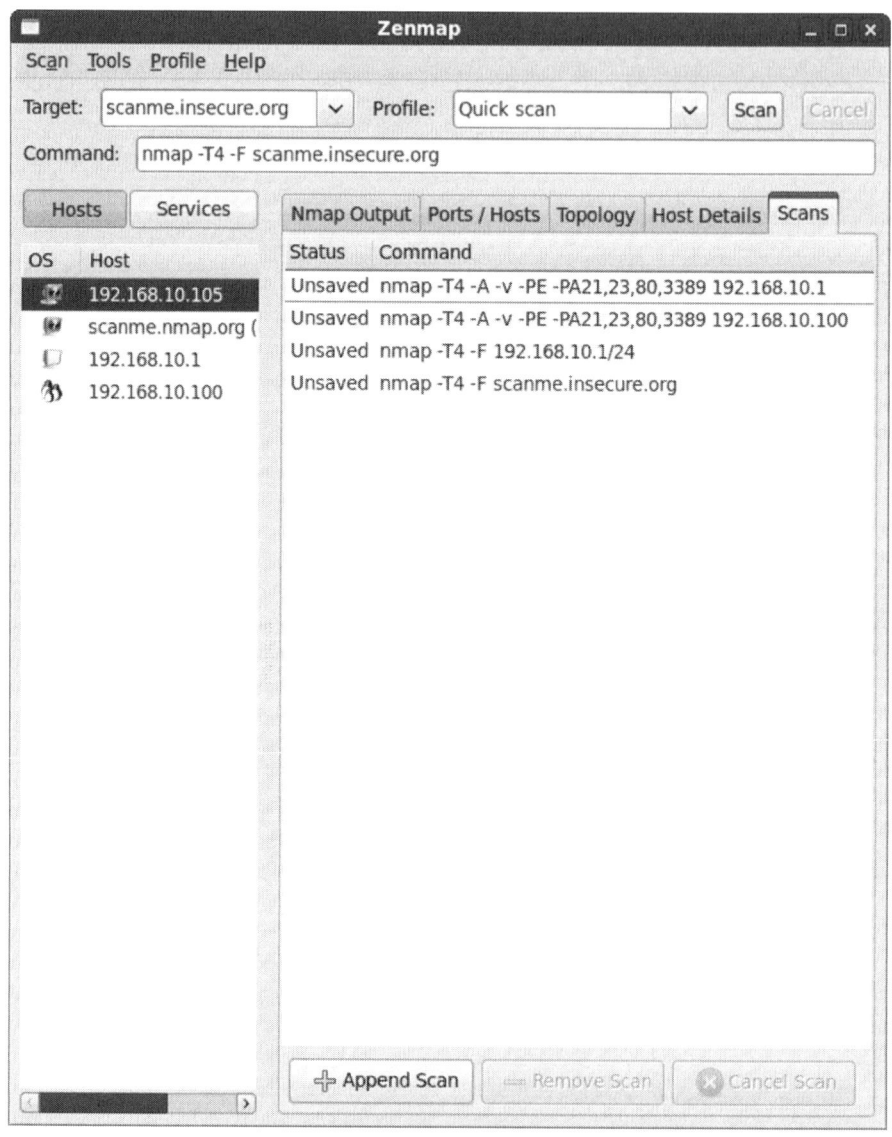

Zenmap scan history

Comparing Scan Results

Nmap and Zenmap scans can be compared using the **Compare Results** function. To do this, select **Tools > Compare Results** from the Zenmap menu or press **CTRL + D**.

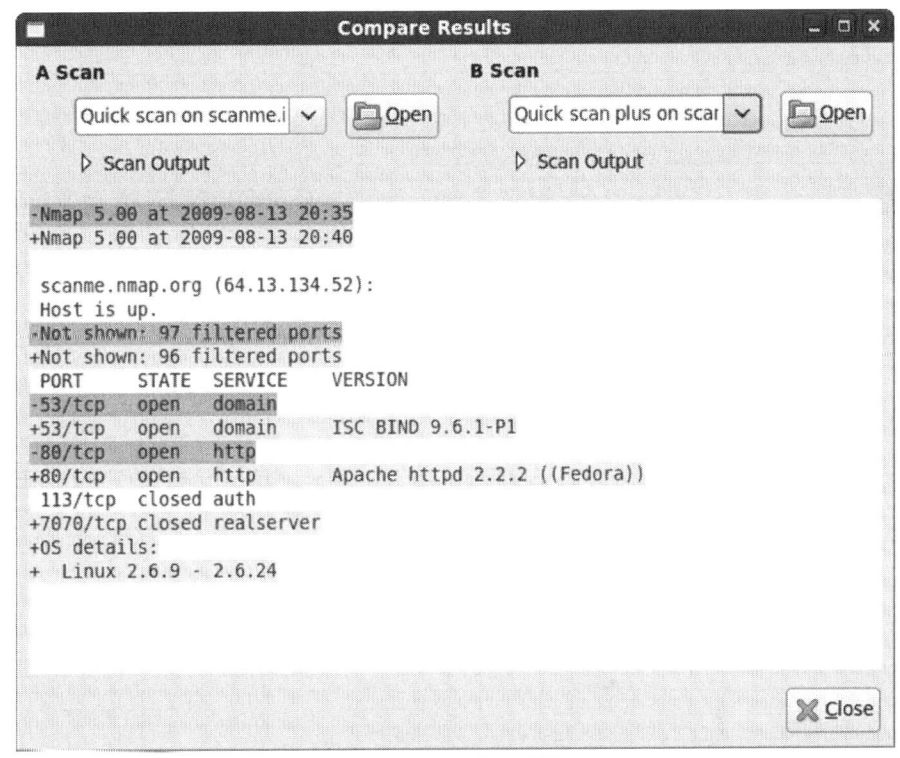

```
                        Compare Results                         _ □ x
 A Scan                          B Scan
 [Quick scan on scanme.i ∨]  [ Open ]  [Quick scan plus on scar ∨]  [ Open ]
   ▷ Scan Output                  ▷ Scan Output

-Nmap 5.00 at 2009-08-13 20:35
+Nmap 5.00 at 2009-08-13 20:40

 scanme.nmap.org (64.13.134.52):
 Host is up.
-Not shown: 97 filtered ports
+Not shown: 96 filtered ports
 PORT       STATE  SERVICE    VERSION
-53/tcp     open   domain
+53/tcp     open   domain     ISC BIND 9.6.1-P1
-80/tcp     open   http
+80/tcp     open   http       Apache httpd 2.2.2 ((Fedora))
 113/tcp    closed auth
+7070/tcp   closed realserver
+OS details:
+  Linux 2.6.9 - 2.6.24

                                                          [ ✕ Close ]
```

Zenmap comparison utility

Zenmap will load recent scans into the comparison utility or you can import an Nmap XML file (discussed on page 130) by pressing the **Open** button. The differences between the two selected scans are highlighted for easy comparison.

159

Saving Scans

Zenmap scans can be saved for future reference by selecting **Scan > Save Scan** from the menu or pressing **CTRL + S**.

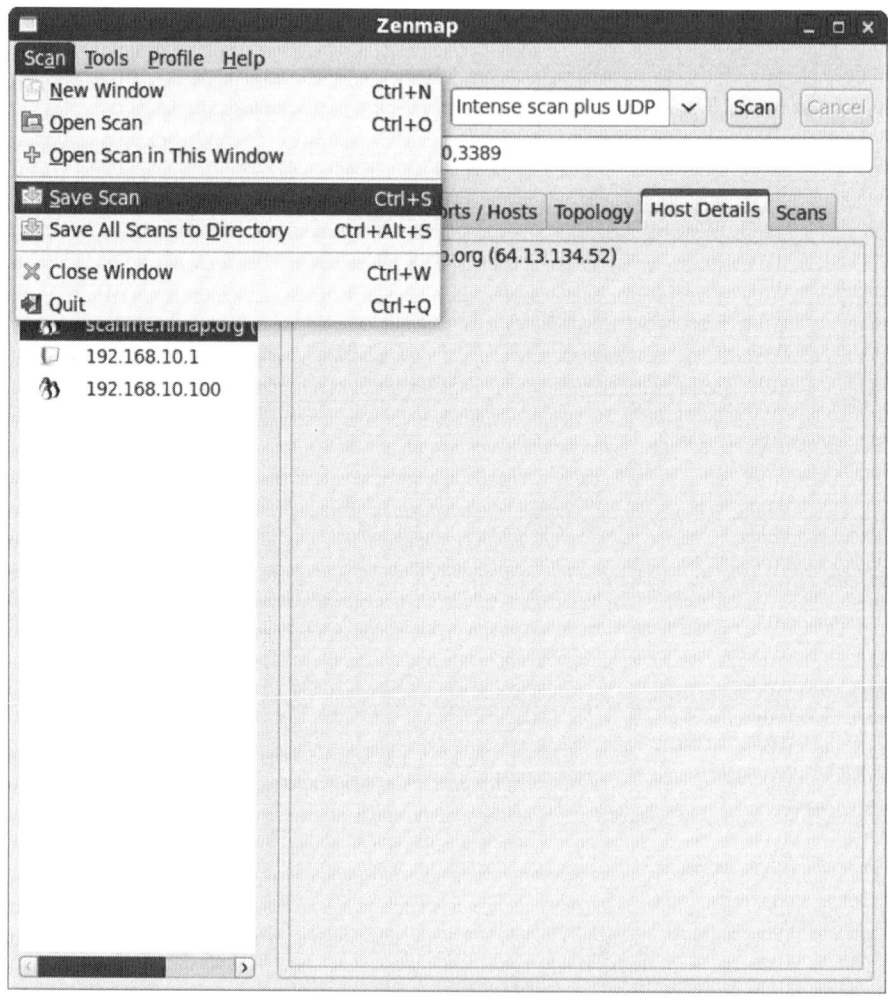

Saving Zenmap scans

Section 12:

Nmap Scripting Engine (NSE)

Nmap Scripting Engine Overview

The Nmap Scripting Engine (NSE) is a powerful tool that allows users to develop custom scripts which can be used to harness Nmap's advanced scanning functions. In addition to the ability to write your own custom scripts, there are also a number of standard built-in scripts that offer some interesting features such as vulnerability detection and exploitation. This section covers the basic usage of these built-in scripts.

> **Note:** Scripts for NSE are written in the Lua programming language. Unfortunately, programming in Lua is outside the scope of this book. For more information about Lua visit www.lua.org.

> **Warning:** The NSE uses aggressive scanning techniques which (in some rare cases) can cause undesirable results like system downtime and data loss. Additionally, NSE vulnerability exploitation features could get you into legal trouble if you don't have permission to scan the target systems

Summary of features covered in this section:

Feature	Option
Execute Individual Scripts	--script [script]
Execute Multiple Scripts	--script [script1,script2,etc]
Execute Scripts by Category	--script [category]
Execute Multiple Script Categories	--script [category1, category2]
Troubleshoot Scripts	--script-trace
Update the Script Database	--script-updatedb

Execute Individual Scripts

The **--script** argument is used to execute NSE scripts.

Usage syntax: nmap --script [script.nse] [target]

```
# nmap --script whois.nse scanme.insecure.org

Starting Nmap 5.00 ( http://nmap.org ) at 2009-11-13 15:27 CST
Interesting ports on scanme.nmap.org (64.13.134.52):
Not shown: 996 filtered ports
PORT      STATE   SERVICE
25/tcp    closed  smtp
53/tcp    open    domain
70/tcp    closed  gopher
80/tcp    open    http

Host script results:
|  whois: Record found at whois.arin.net
|  netrange: 64.13.134.0 - 64.13.134.63
|  netname: NET-64-13-143-0-26
|  orgname: Titan Networks
|  orgid: INSEC
|_ country: US stateprov: CA

Nmap done: 1 IP address (1 host up) scanned in 8.12 seconds
```

Executing a NSE script

Script results are displayed under the heading "Host script results". In the example above, the **--script** option is used to execute a script called whois.nse. The built-in whois.nse script retrieves information about the public IP address of the specified target from ARIN (American Registry for Internet Numbers). This is just one of the many built-in NSE scripts.

> **Tip** *A complete list of the built-in scripts for Nmap 5.00 can be found online at www.nmap.org/nsedoc/.*

Execute Multiple Scripts

The Nmap Scripting Engine supports the ability to run multiple scripts concurrently.

Usage syntax: nmap --script [script1,script2,etc|"expression"] [target]

```
# nmap --script "smtp*" 10.10.1.44

Starting Nmap 5.00 ( http://nmap.org ) at 2009-11-15 14:24 CST
Interesting ports on 10.10.1.44:
...
|  smtp-commands: EHLO exchange-01.dontfearthecommandline.com Hello
[10.10.1.173], TURN, SIZE, ETRN, PIPELINING, DSN, ENHANCEDSTATUSCODES,
8bitmime, BINARYMIME, CHUNKING, VRFY, X-EXPS GSSAPI NTLM LOGIN, X-
EXPS=LOGIN, AUTH GSSAPI NTLM LOGIN, AUTH=LOGIN, X-LINK2STATE, XEXCH50
|_ HELP This server supports the following commands: HELO EHLO
STARTTLS RCPT DATA RSET MAIL QUIT HELP AUTH TURN ETRN BDAT VRFY
|_ smtp-open-relay: OPEN RELAY found.
...
```

Executing all SMTP scripts

In this example, the asterisks wildcard character is used to execute all scripts that begin with *smtp*. You can also provide a comma-separated list of individual scripts to run using the following syntax: **nmap --script script1,script2,script3,etc.**

Note	When using wildcards, the expression must be enclosed in quotes such as *"smtp*"* or *"ftp*"*.

Tip	Some Nmap scripts accept arguments using the **--script-args** option. This allows you to specify specific parameters for a script. A complete list of arguments for each script can be found at www.nmap.org/nsedoc/.

Script Categories

You can use the **--script** option to execute NSE scripts based on category. The table below describes the available categories:

Categories	Purpose
all	Runs all available NSE scripts
auth	Scripts related to authentication
default	Runs a basic set of default scripts
discovery	Attempts to discover in depth information about a target
external	Scripts that contact external sources (such as the whois database)
intrusive	Scripts which may be considered intrusive by the target system
malware	Scripts that check for open backdoors and malware
safe	Basic scripts that are not intrusive
vuln	Checks target for commonly exploited vulnerabilities

NSE script categories

Using script categories is the easiest way to launch NSE built-in scripts – unless you know the specific script you want to run. Executing scripts by category, however, can take longer to complete since each category contains numerous scripts.

> **Tip**: A complete list of the NSE scripts in each category can be found online at www.nmap.org/nsedoc/.

Execute Scripts by Category

The **--script** option can be used to execute multiple scripts based on their category.

Usage syntax: nmap --script [category] [target]

```
# nmap --script default 10.10.1.70

Starting Nmap 5.00 ( http://nmap.org ) at 2009-11-13 15:09 CST
Interesting ports on 10.10.1.70:
Not shown: 997 filtered ports
PORT        STATE   SERVICE
139/tcp     open    netbios-ssn
445/tcp     open    microsoft-ds
5900/tcp    open    vnc
MAC Address: 00:0C:F1:A6:1F:16 (Intel)

Host script results:
|_ nbstat: NetBIOS name: AXIS-01, NetBIOS user: <unknown>, NetBIOS
MAC: 00:0c:f1:a6:1f:16
|  smb-os-discovery: Windows XP
|  LAN Manager: Windows 2000 LAN Manager
|  Name: WORKGROUP\AXIS-01
|_ System time: 2009-11-13 15:09:12 UTC-6

Nmap done: 1 IP address (1 host up) scanned in 52.40 seconds
```

Executing all scripts in the default category

By specifying a category (see page 165) with the **--script** option Nmap will execute every script in that category. In the example above, the results of the scripts in the default category are displayed under the *"Host script results"* heading.

> **Tip**
> The *-sC* option is a shortcut for **--script default** which will execute all of the NSE scripts in the default category.

Execute Multiple Script Categories

Multiple script categories can be executed concurrently using one of the following syntax structures:

`nmap --script category1,category2,etc`
Specifying multiple script categories as a comma-separated list would execute all scripts in the defined categories. For example, executing `nmap --script malware,vuln` would run all scripts in the malware and vulnerabilities categories.

`nmap --script "category1 and category2"`
NSE scripts can belong to more than one category. Using this syntax would execute all that belong to both the specified categories. For example, `nmap --script "default and safe"` would only execute scripts that belong to both the default *and* safe categories.

`nmap --script "category1 or category2"`
The *or* operator can be used to run scripts that belong to either of the specified categories. For example, `nmap --script "default or safe"` would execute all scripts that belong to either the default *or* safe categories.

`nmap --script "not category"`
The *not* operator is used to exclude scripts that belong to the specified category. For example, executing `nmap --script "not intrusive"` would run all scripts that do not belong to the intrusive category.

Troubleshoot Scripts

The **--script-trace** option is used to trace NSE scripts.

Usage syntax: `nmap --script [script(s)] --script-trace [target]`

```
# nmap --script default --script-trace 10.10.1.70
Starting Nmap 5.00 ( http://nmap.org ) at 2009-11-14 13:51 CST
NSOCK (5.1060s) nsock_loop() started (timeout=50ms). 0 events pending
NSOCK (5.1060s) UDP connection requested to 10.10.1.70:137 (IOD #1) EID 8
NSOCK (5.1070s) TCP connection requested to 10.10.1.70:5900 (IOD #2) EID 16
NSOCK (5.1070s) UDP connection requested to 10.10.1.70:137 (IOD #3) EID 24
NSOCK (5.1080s) nsock_loop() started (timeout=50ms). 3 events pending
NSOCK (5.1080s) Callback: CONNECT SUCCESS for EID 8 [10.10.1.70:137]
NSE: UDP 10.10.1.173:56824 > 10.10.1.70:137 | CONNECT
NSOCK (5.1080s) Callback: CONNECT SUCCESS for EID 16 [10.10.1.70:5900]
NSE: TCP 10.10.1.173:49401 > 10.10.1.70:5900 | CONNECT
NSOCK (5.1080s) Callback: CONNECT SUCCESS for EID 24 [10.10.1.70:137]
...
```

NSE trace output

The **--script-trace** option displays all packets sent and received by an NSE script and is useful for troubleshooting problems related to scripts.

Some scripts can generate thousands of lines of output when using the script trace option. In most cases, it is better to redirect the output to a file for later review. The example below demonstrates how to do this.

```
# nmap --script default 10.10.1.70 --script-trace > trace.txt
```

Redirecting the output of a NSE trace

The resulting trace.txt file will contain all of the trace data and can be viewed in a standard text editor.

Update the Script Database

The **--script-updatedb** option is used to update the script database.

Usage syntax: `nmap --script-updatedb`

```
# nmap --script-updatedb

Starting Nmap 5.00 ( http://nmap.org ) at 2009-11-14 13:42 CST
NSE: Updating rule database.
NSE script database updated successfully.
Nmap done: 0 IP addresses (0 hosts up) scanned in 0.38 seconds
```
Updating the NSE script database

Nmap maintains a database of scripts that is used to facilitate the option of executing multiple scripts via category (discussed on page 164). Most Unix-like systems store scripts in the **/usr/share/nmap/scripts/** directory. Windows systems store these files in **C:\Program Files\Nmap\scripts**. If you add or remove scripts from the scripts directory you must run **nmap --script-updatedb** to apply the changes to the script database.

Section 13:

Ndiff

Ndiff Overview

Ndiff is a tool within the Nmap suite that allows you to compare two scans and flag any changes between them. It accepts two Nmap XML output files (discussed on page 130) and highlights the differences between each file for easy comparison. Ndiff can be used on the command line or in GUI form within the Zenmap application (see page 159).

Summary of features covered in this section:

Feature	Option
Comparison Using Ndiff	ndiff
Ndiff Verbose Mode	-v
XML Output Mode	--xml

Scan Comparison Using Ndiff

The **ndiff** utility is used to perform a comparison of two Nmap scans.

Usage syntax: `ndiff [file1.xml file2.xml]`

```
# ndiff scan1.xml scan2.xml
-Nmap 5.00 at 2009-12-17 09:18
+Nmap 5.00 at 2009-12-18 12:44

 10.10.1.48, 00:0C:29:D5:38:F4:
-Not shown: 994 closed ports
+Not shown: 995 closed ports
 PORT    STATE SERVICE VERSION
-80/tcp  open  http
```

Comparison of two Nmap scans

Basic usage of the Ndiff utility consists of comparing two Nmap XML output files (discussed on page 130). Differences between the two files are highlighted with a minus sign indicating the information in the first file and the plus sign indicating the changes within the second file. In the above example we see that port 80 on the second scan has changed states from *open* to *closed*.

Ndiff Verbose Mode

The **-v** option is used to display verbose output with Ndiff.

Usage syntax: ndiff -v [file1.xml file2.xml]
```
# ndiff -v scan1.xml scan2.xml
-Nmap 5.00 at 2009-12-17 09:18
+Nmap 5.00 at 2009-12-18 12:44

 10.10.1.48, 00:0C:29:D5:38:F4:
 Host is up.
-Not shown: 994 closed ports
+Not shown: 995 closed ports
 PORT      STATE SERVICE VERSION
 21/tcp    open  ftp
 22/tcp    open  ssh
 25/tcp    open  smtp
-80/tcp    open  http
 111/tcp   open  rpcbind
 2049/tcp  open  nfs
```

Output of a Ndiff scan in verbose mode

The verbose output displays all lines of both XML files and highlights the differences with a minus sign indicating the information in the first file and the plus sign indicating the changes within the second file. This is in contrast to the default Ndiff behavior (described on page 173) which only displays the differences between the two files. Verbose output is often more helpful than the default output as it displays all information from the original scan.

XML Output Mode

The **-xml** option is used to generate XML output with Ndiff.

Usage syntax: ndiff --xml [file1.xml] [file2.xml]

```
# ndiff --xml scan1.xml scan2.xml
<?xml version="1.0" encoding="UTF-8"?>
<nmapdiff version="1">
  <scandiff>
    <hostdiff>
      <host>
        <address addr="10.10.1.48" addrtype="ipv4"/>
        <address addr="00:0C:29:D5:38:F4" addrtype="mac"/>
        <ports>
          <a>
            <extraports count="994" state="closed"/>
          </a>
          <b>
            <extraports count="995" state="closed"/>
          </b>
          <portdiff>
            <a>
              <port portid="80" protocol="tcp">
                <state state="open"/>
                <service name="http"/>
...
```

Ndiff XML output

XML output is a great tool for feeding information from Ndiff into a third party program using a widely supported format.

> **Tip**
> The default **--xml** output displays the XML code on the screen. To save this information file, type **ndiff --xml scan1.xml scan2.xml >ndiff.xml** which will redirect the output to a file called ndiff.xml.

Section 14:

Tips and Tricks

Tips and Tricks Overview

This section provides several helpful tips and tricks for getting the most out of Nmap. It also incorporates the use of third party programs that work in conjunction with Nmap to help you analyze your network.

Summary of topics discussed in this section:

Topic	Page
Combine Multiple Options	179
Scan Using Interactive Mode	180
Runtime Interaction	181
Remotely Scan Your Network	182
Wireshark	183
Scanme.Insecure.org	184
Nmap Online Resources	185

Combine Multiple Options

If you haven't already noticed, Nmap allows you to combine multiple options to produce a custom scan unique to your needs.

Usage syntax: nmap [options] [target]

```
# nmap --reason -F --open -T3 -O scanme.insecure.org

Starting Nmap 5.00 ( http://nmap.org ) at 2009-12-17 16:01 CST
Interesting ports on scanme.nmap.org (64.13.134.52):
Not shown: 95 filtered ports, 3 closed ports
Reason: 95 no-responses and 3 resets
PORT    STATE SERVICE REASON
53/tcp  open  domain  syn-ack
80/tcp  open  http    syn-ack
Device type: general purpose|WAP|firewall|router
Running (JUST GUESSING) : Linux 2.6.X|2.4.X (95%), Linksys Linux 2.4.X
...
```

Combining multiple Nmap options

In the above example, many different options are combined to produce the desired results. As you can see, the possibilities are nearly limitless. You should note, however, that not all options are compatible with each other, as illustrated in the next example.

```
# nmap -PN -sP 10.10.1.*
-PN (skip ping) is incompatible with -sP (ping scan). If you only
want to enumerate hosts, try list scan (-sL)
```

Nmap warning with combining incompatible options

In this example, the **-PN** option (don't ping) and **-sP** option (ping only) are obviously not compatible with each other. Fortunately, Nmap provides a friendly and informative error message and thus no harm is done.

Scan Using Interactive Mode

The **--interactive** option enables the Nmap interactive shell.

Usage syntax: nmap --interactive

```
$ nmap --interactive

Starting Nmap V. 5.00 ( http://nmap.org )
Welcome to Interactive Mode -- press h <enter> for help
nmap>
```
Nmap interactive mode shell

Once in interactive mode, you can launch a scan by simply typing the letter **n** followed by the target address and any standard Nmap options. The example below demonstrates using interactive mode to perform a simple **-F** scan.

Usage syntax: n [options] [target]

```
nmap> n -F 10.10.1.1
Interesting ports on 10.10.1.1:
Not shown: 98 closed ports
PORT     STATE SERVICE
80/tcp   open  http
443/tcp  open  https

Nmap done: 1 IP address (1 host up) scanned in 0.19 seconds
```
Example scan using Nmap in interactive mode

When you are done scanning, simply type **x** to exit the interactive shell.

Tip	*Pressing the **h** key in interactive mode displays a help menu which describes the available options.*

Runtime Interaction

Nmap offers several runtime interaction keystrokes that can modify an in progress scan. The table below lists Nmap's runtime interaction keys.

Key	Function
v	Pressing lowercase **v** during a scan will increase the verbosity level.
V	Pressing uppercase **V** during a scan will increase the verbosity level.
d	Pressing lowercase **d** during a scan will increase the debugging level.
D	Pressing uppercase **D** during a scan will increase the debugging level.
p	Pressing lowercase **p** during a scan will enable packet tracing.
P	Pressing uppercase **P** during a scan will disable packet tracing.
?	Pressing **?** during a scan will display the runtime interaction help.
Any other key not listed above	Pressing key other than the ones defined above during a scan will print a status message indicating the progress of the scan and how much time is remaining.

Nmap runtime interaction keys

Runtime interaction is very useful getting status updates when performing a scan on a large number of hosts. The example below displays the status of the current scan when the space bar pressed.

```
# nmap -T2 10.10.1.*
[space]
Stats: 0:06:45 elapsed; 18 hosts completed (30 up), 30 undergoing SYN
Stealth Scan
SYN Stealth Scan Timing: About 38.44% done; ETC: 16:56 (0:10:26
remaining)
...
```

Using runtime interaction keys to display scan status

In addition to being able to display status updates, run time interaction keys can also adjust verbosity, tracing, and debugging settings without interrupting the scan in progress.

Remotely Scan Your Network

Nmap Online is a website that provides (free) Nmap scanning functionality via a web browser. This can be useful for remotely scanning your network or troubleshooting connectivity problems from an external source. Simply visit **www.nmap-online.com** and enter your IP address or the address of the target system you wish to scan.

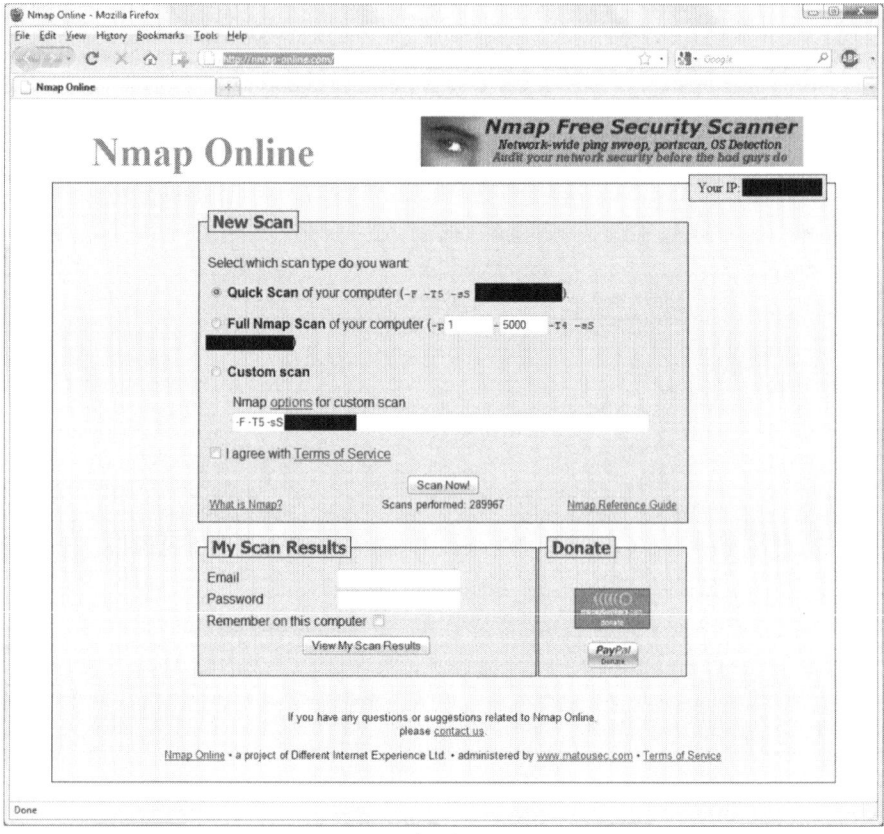

Nmap online home page

Note: To prevent abuse, Nmap Online allows a maximum of 5 scan requests from one IP address every 24 hours and a maximum of 20 scans every 7 days. You must also agree with the terms of service before you can execute a scan.

Wireshark

Wireshark is an excellent addition to any system administrator's toolkit. It is a sophisticated (yet easy to use) network protocol analyzer. You can use Wireshark to capture and analyze network traffic and it works hand in hand with Nmap allowing you to see each packet sent and received while scanning.

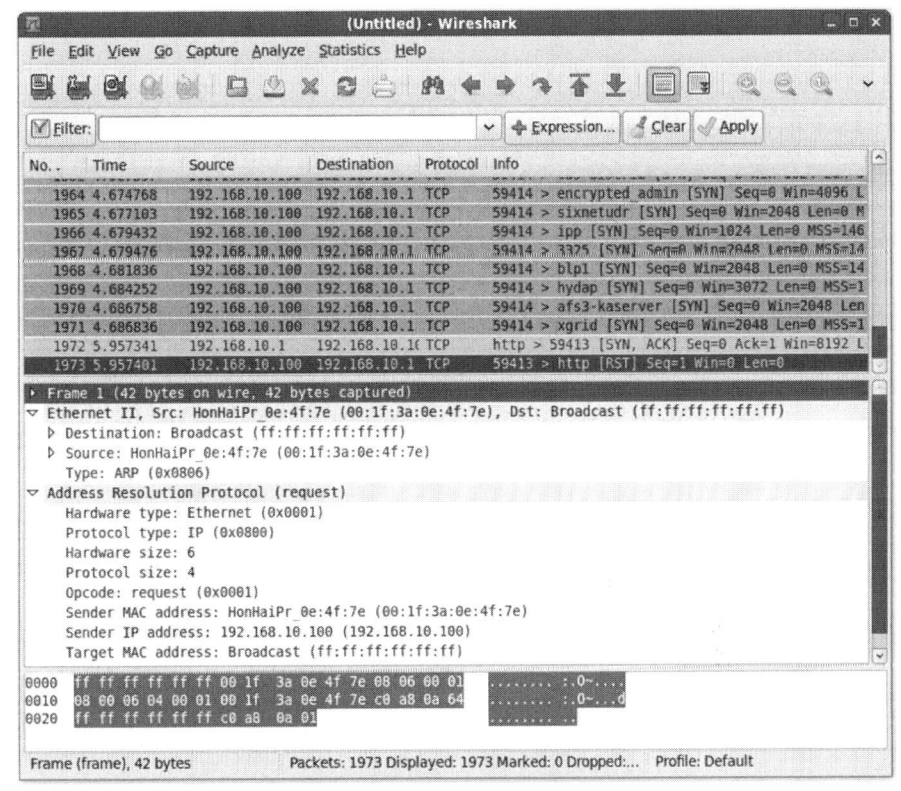

Wireshark network protocol analyzer

Wireshark is available for Windows, Linux, and Mac OS X and can be downloaded for free at www.wireshark.org.

Scanme.Insecure.org

The scanme.insecure.org server is a common example target used throughout this guide. This system is hosted by the Nmap project and can be freely scanned by Nmap users.

```
# nmap -F scanme.insecure.org

Starting Nmap 5.00 ( http://nmap.org ) at 2009-12-18 16:52 CST
Interesting ports on scanme.nmap.org (64.13.134.52):
Not shown: 95 filtered ports
PORT     STATE  SERVICE
25/tcp   closed smtp
53/tcp   open   domain
80/tcp   open   http
110/tcp  closed pop3
113/tcp  closed auth

Nmap done: 1 IP address (1 host up) scanned in 2.63 seconds
```

Example scan using scanme.insecure.org as the target

> **Note** *The good people of the Nmap project provide this valuable service as an education and troubleshooting tool and request that you be polite by not aggressively scanning it hundreds of times a day or with other tools not related to Nmap.*

Nmap Online Resources

Fyodor's Nmap Book
www.nmap.org/book/man.html

Nmap Install Guide
www.nmap.org/book/install.html

Nmap Scripting Engine Documentation
www.nmap.org/nsedoc/

Zenmap Reference Guide
www.nmap.org/book/zenmap.html

Nmap Change Log
www.nmap.org/changelog.html

Nmap Mailing Lists
www.seclists.org

Nmap Online Scan
www.nmap-online.com

Security Tools
www.sectools.org

Nmap Mailing Lists
www.seclists.org

Nmap Facebook
www.nmap.org/fb

Nmap Twitter
www.twitter.com/nmap

Nmap Cookbook
www.nmapcookbook.com

Appendix A - Nmap Cheat Sheet

Download and print this cheat sheet online at www.NmapCookbook.com

Basic Scanning Techniques	
Scan a Single Target	`nmap [target]`
Scan Multiple Targets	`nmap [target1, target2, etc]`
Scan a List of Targets	`nmap -iL [list.txt]`
Scan a Range of Hosts	`nmap [range of ip addresses]`
Scan an Entire Subnet	`nmap [ip address/cdir]`
Scan Random Hosts	`nmap -iR [number]`
Excluding Targets from a Scan	`nmap [targets] --exclude [targets]`
Excluding Targets Using a List	`nmap [targets] --excludefile [list.txt]`
Perform an Aggressive Scan	`nmap -A [target]`
Scan an IPv6 Target	`nmap -6 [target]`
Discovery Options	
Perform a Ping Only Scan	`nmap -sP [target]`
Don't Ping	`nmap -PN [target]`
TCP SYN Ping	`nmap -PS [target]`
TCP ACK Ping	`nmap -PA [target]`
UDP Ping	`nmap -PU [target]`
SCTP INIT Ping	`nmap -PY [target]`
ICMP Echo Ping	`nmap -PE [target]`
ICMP Timestamp Ping	`nmap -PP [target]`
ICMP Address Mask Ping	`nmap -PM [target]`
IP Protocol Ping	`nmap -PO [target]`
ARP Ping	`nmap -PR [target]`
Traceroute	`nmap --traceroute [target]`
Force Reverse DNS Resolution	`nmap -R [target]`
Disable Reverse DNS Resolution	`nmap -n [target]`
Alternative DNS Lookup	`nmap --system-dns [target]`
Manually Specify DNS Server(s)	`nmap --dns-servers [servers] [target]`
Create a Host List	`nmap -sL [targets]`
Advanced Scanning Functions	
TCP SYN Scan	`nmap -sS [target]`
TCP Connect Scan	`nmap -sT [target]`
UDP Scan	`nmap -sU [target]`
TCP NULL Scan	`nmap -sN [target]`
TCP FIN Scan	`nmap -sF [target]`
Xmas Scan	`nmap -sX [target]`
TCP ACK Scan	`nmap -sA [target]`
Custom TCP Scan	`nmap --scanflags [flags] [target]`
IP Protocol Scan	`nmap -sO [target]`
Send Raw Ethernet Packets	`nmap --send-eth [target]`
Send IP Packets	`nmap --send-ip [target]`

Port Scanning Options	
Perform a Fast Scan	`nmap -F [target]`
Scan Specific Ports	`nmap -p [port(s)] [target]`
Scan Ports by Name	`nmap -p [port name(s)] [target]`
Scan Ports by Protocol	`nmap -sU -sT -p U:[ports],T:[ports] [target]`
Scan All Ports	`nmap -p "*" [target]`
Scan Top Ports	`nmap --top-ports [number] [target]`
Perform a Sequential Port Scan	`nmap -r [target]`
Version Detection	
Operating System Detection	`nmap -O [target]`
Submit TCP/IP Fingerprints	`www.nmap.org/submit/`
Attempt to Guess an Unknown	`nmap -O --osscan-guess [target]`
Service Version Detection	`nmap -sV [target]`
Troubleshooting Version Scans	`nmap -sV --version-trace [target]`
Perform a RPC Scan	`nmap -sR [target]`
Timing Options	
Timing Templates	`nmap -T[0-5] [target]`
Set the Packet TTL	`nmap --ttl [time] [target]`
Minimum # of Parallel Operations	`nmap --min-parallelism [number] [target]`
Maximum # of Parallel Operations	`nmap --max-parallelism [number] [target]`
Minimum Host Group Size	`nmap --min-hostgroup [number] [targets]`
Maximum Host Group Size	`nmap --max-hostgroup [number] [targets]`
Maximum RTT Timeout	`nmap --initial-rtt-timeout [time] [target]`
Initial RTT Timeout	`nmap --max-rtt-timeout [TTL] [target]`
Maximum Retries	`nmap --max-retries [number] [target]`
Host Timeout	`nmap --host-timeout [time] [target]`
Minimum Scan Delay	`nmap --scan-delay [time] [target]`
Maximum Scan Delay	`nmap --max-scan-delay [time] [target]`
Minimum Packet Rate	`nmap --min-rate [number] [target]`
Maximum Packet Rate	`nmap --max-rate [number] [target]`
Defeat Reset Rate Limits	`nmap --defeat-rst-ratelimit [target]`
Firewall Evasion Techniques	
Fragment Packets	`nmap -f [target]`
Specify a Specific MTU	`nmap --mtu [MTU] [target]`
Use a Decoy	`nmap -D RND:[number] [target]`
Idle Zombie Scan	`nmap -sI [zombie] [target]`
Manually Specify a Source Port	`nmap --source-port [port] [target]`
Append Random Data	`nmap --data-length [size] [target]`
Randomize Target Scan Order	`nmap --randomize-hosts [target]`
Spoof MAC Address	`nmap --spoof-mac [MAC|0|vendor] [target]`
Send Bad Checksums	`nmap --badsum [target]`

Output Options	
Save Output to a Text File	`nmap -oN [scan.txt] [target]`
Save Output to a XML File	`nmap -oX [scan.xml] [target]`
Grepable Output	`nmap -oG [scan.txt] [targets]`
Output All Supported File Types	`nmap -oA [path/filename] [target]`
Periodically Display Statistics	`nmap --stats-every [time] [target]`
133t Output	`nmap -oS [scan.txt] [target]`
Troubleshooting and Debugging	
Getting Help	`nmap -h`
Display Nmap Version	`nmap -V`
Verbose Output	`nmap -v [target]`
Debugging	`nmap -d [target]`
Display Port State Reason	`nmap --reason [target]`
Only Display Open Ports	`nmap --open [target]`
Trace Packets	`nmap --packet-trace [target]`
Display Host Networking	`nmap --iflist`
Specify a Network Interface	`nmap -e [interface] [target]`
Nmap Scripting Engine	
Execute Individual Scripts	`nmap --script [script.nse] [target]`
Execute Multiple Scripts	`nmap --script [expression] [target]`
Script Categories	`all, auth, default, discovery, external, intrusive, malware, safe, vuln`
Execute Scripts by Category	`nmap --script [category] [target]`
Execute Multiple Script Categories	`nmap --script [category1,category2,etc]`
Troubleshoot Scripts	`nmap --script [script] --script-trace [target]`
Update the Script Database	`nmap --script-updatedb`
Ndiff	
Comparison Using Ndiff	`ndiff [scan1.xml] [scan2.xml]`
Ndiff Verbose Mode	`ndiff -v [scan1.xml] [scan2.xml]`
XML Output Mode	`ndiff --xml [scan1.xml] [scan2.xml]`

Appendix B - Nmap Port States

open

An open port is a port that actively responds to an incoming connection.

closed

A closed port is a port on a target that actively responds to a probe but does not have any service running on the port. Closed ports are commonly found on systems where no firewall is in place to filter incoming traffic.

filtered

Filtered ports are ports that are typically protected by a firewall of some sort that prevents Nmap from determining whether or not the port is open or closed.

unfiltered

An unfiltered port is a port that Nmap can access but is unable to determine whether it is open or closed.

open|filtered

An open|filtered port is a port which Nmap believes to be open or filtered but cannot determine which exact state the port is actually in.

closed|filtered

A closed|filtered port is a port that Nmap believes to be closed or filtered but cannot determine which respective state the port is actually in.

Appendix C - CIDR Cross Reference

Subnet Mask	CIDR
000.000.000.000	/0
128.000.000.000	/1
192.000.000.000	/2
224.000.000.000	/3
240.000.000.000	/4
248.000.000.000	/5
252.000.000.000	/6
254.000.000.000	/7
255.000.000.000	/8
255.128.000.000	/9
255.192.000.000	/10
255.224.000.000	/11
255.240.000.000	/12
255.248.000.000	/13
255.252.000.000	/14
255.254.000.000	/15
255.255.000.000	/16
255.255.128.000	/17
255.255.192.000	/18
255.255.224.000	/19
255.255.240.000	/20
255.255.248.000	/21
255.255.252.000	/22
255.255.254.000	/23
255.255.255.000	/24
255.255.255.128	/25
255.255.255.192	/26
255.255.255.224	/27
255.255.255.240	/28
255.255.255.248	/29
255.255.255.252	/30
255.255.255.254	/31
255.255.255.255	/32

Appendix D - Common TCP/IP Ports

Port	Type	Usage
20	TCP	FTP Data
21	TCP	FTP Control
22	TCP|UDP	Secure Shell (SSH)
23	TCP	Telnet
25	TCP	Simple Mail Transfer Protocol (SMTP)
42	TCP|UDP	Windows Internet Name Service (WINS)
53	TCP|UDP	Domain Name System (DNS)
67	UDP	DHCP Server
68	UDP	DHCP Client
69	UDP	Trivial File Transfer Protocol (TFTP)
80	TCP|UDP	Hypertext Transfer Protocol (HTTP)
110	TCP	Post Office Protocol 3 (POP3)
119	TCP	Network News Transfer Protocol (NNTP)
123	UDP	Network Time Protocol (NTP)
135	TCP|UDP	Microsoft RPC
137	TCP|UDP	NetBIOS Name Service
138	TCP|UDP	NetBIOS Datagram Service
139	TCP|UDP	NetBIOS Session Service
143	TCP|UDP	Internet Message Access Protocol (IMAP)
161	TCP|UDP	Simple Network Management Protocol (SNMP)
162	TCP|UDP	Simple Network Management Protocol (SNMP) Trap
389	TCP|UDP	Lightweight Directory Access Protocol (LDAP)
443	TCP|UDP	Hypertext Transfer Protocol over TLS/SSL (HTTPS)
445	TCP	Server Message Block (SMB)
636	TCP|UDP	Lightweight Directory Access Protocol over TLS/SSL (LDAPS)
873	TCP	Remote File Synchronization Protocol (rsync)
993	TCP	Internet Message Access Protocol over SSL (IMAPS)
995	TCP	Post Office Protocol 3 over TLS/SSL (POP3S)
1433	TCP	Microsoft SQL Server Database
3306	TCP	MySQL Database
3389	TCP	Microsoft Terminal Server/Remote Desktop Protocol (RDP)
5800	TCP	Virtual Network Computing (VNC) web interface
5900	TCP	Virtual Network Computing (VNC) remote desktop

Ready to learn the command line?

Check out our latest title...

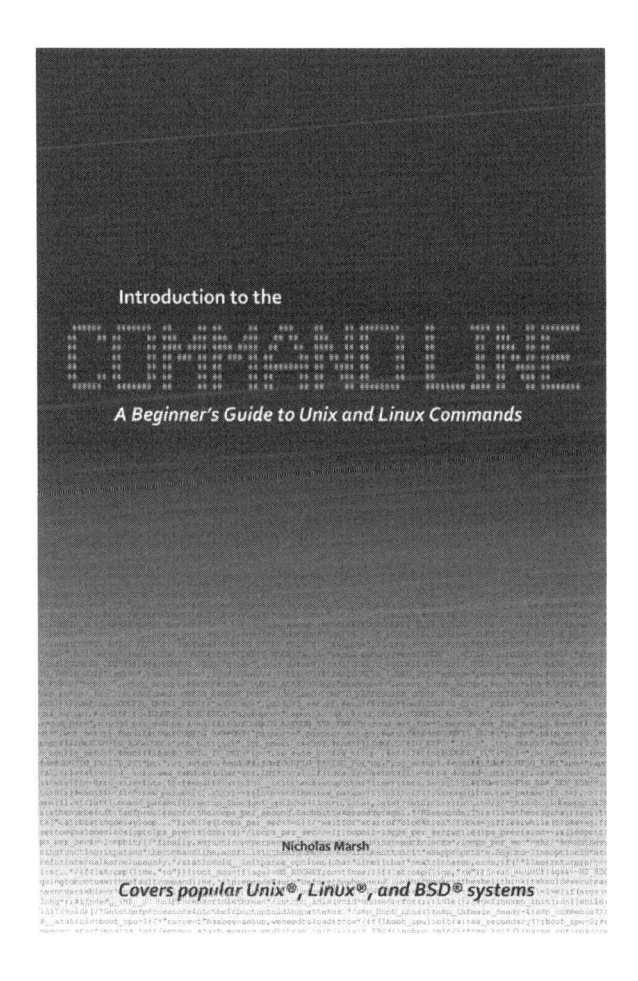

Introduction to the Command Line is a practical guide that teaches the most important Unix and Linux shell commands in a simple and straightforward manner. All command line programs covered are presented with visual examples to aid in the learning process and help you master the command line quickly and easily.

www.DontFearTheCommandLine.com

Made in the USA
San Bernardino, CA
18 November 2012